THE MAKING OF A MINISTER

THE AUTOBIOGRAPHY OF

CLARENCE E. MACARTNEY

THE
MAKING
OF A
MINISTER

Edited and with an introduction by J. Clyde Henry

Foreword by Frank E. Gaebelein

PUBLISHED BY
CHANNEL PRESS, INC.,
GREAT NECK, NEW YORK

TO

Ruth, Etta, and Edith

FELLOW-LABORERS IN THE GOSPEL

TABLE OF CONTENTS

FOREWORD

ONE of the marks of these confused and complicated times is
the growing concern for the definition of our national purpose: not only the might of a disciplined Soviet Union, but
also a revulsion against the softness of a pleasure-loving and
materialistic age, has stimulated a spirit of self-criticism on
the part of many thoughtful Americans. The author of *The
Making of a Minister* died before the present discussion of
the national purpose began. Nevertheless, as pastor of a great
city church, Clarence Edward Macartney knew the problems and trends of the day. And his plain and unpretentious
autobiography speaks to our situation and will continue to
speak to our successors, because it exemplifies certain endur-
ing values on which America is built.

Dr. Macartney was a great preacher, to use an adjective
that in respect to the high calling of the ministry should always be sparingly employed. There was in his preaching a
real measure of grandeur. High seriousness, powerful direct-
ness, intense conviction, mastery of the Scriptures, and
knowledge of the human heart marked his sermons. In his
imaginative illustrations and in his ability to reach the minds
of his listeners he had few equals. A man of sound and broad

education, recognized as an eminent historian, he was above all a Biblical preacher, bringing the resources of knowledge and experience to bear on the communication of the central doctrines of the Scriptures that he might persuade men and women to trust Jesus Christ and lead godly lives. It is a tribute to the discernment of a large number of ministers of various theological points of view that his many volumes of sermons are so widely read.

What, then, is the significance of this autobiography? Obviously it holds a particular appeal for the many who knew and heard or read Dr. Macartney. But its value reaches farther than this. It is a distinguished piece of writing. There is nothing labored in these pages; the style is singularly lacking in self-consciousness. Long and unusual words are at a minimum, yet there is no feeling of narrowness of vocabulary, but rather the impression of an educated man who knows how to go straight to the point.

Moreover, this is a highly interesting book. For students of American Protestantism in the early decades of the twentieth century, Dr. Macartney's account of the fundamentalist-modernist controversy as it came to a focus in Dr. Harry Emerson Fosdick's ministry in the First Presbyterian Church of New York has great historic value. Here is the story of the struggle precipitated by the famous sermon, "Shall the Fundamentalists Win?", told by the chief protagonist on the other side—and thus complementing Dr. Fosdick's account in his own autobiography, *The Living of These Days*. This portion of Dr. Macartney's book should help correct the stereotype of the earlier fundamentalism as merely an obscurantist movement led by men of inferior education. With his training at Pomona College, the University of Wisconsin, and Princeton Theological Seminary, and with his competence as a preacher, Dr. Macartney's opposition to what Dr. Fosdick stood for came not out of ignorance but from a personal con-

viction that the modernist movement threatened the foundations of Biblical Christianity.

Throughout the book are anecdotes told with the skill
we should expect of this master of illustration. The author's
school and college days are sketched in candid and sometimes
humorous detail. Certain passages, such as the description of
the celebration of the Lord's Supper at the Covenanter
Church in Beaver Falls, speak with moving power. Nor will
the reader soon forget the down-to-earth story of the author's
job on a Colorado ranch and the account of the kindness he
experienced in the country parish in Wisconsin where he had
his first preaching assignment. There is sincere emotion in
the book, but nothing of sentimentality, for despite his reputation for aloofness Dr. Macartney's sense of human values
was warm and sturdy.

The reflections upon life come out of wisdom gained
from long experience in dealing with individuals in times of
joy and of sorrow. The evaluations of men and events are
full of understanding, and the wealth of Christian common
sense with which ministerial life and work are treated reveals
much about the author. For an autobiography this is an un-
assuming and in some respects a reticent book. Yet the reader
feels in its quiet dignity the deep sympathy that lay beneath
the author's natural reserve.

Finally, this is a profoundly American book. In a day
when much writing is preoccupied with depravity, and when
the great problems of human life and destiny are portrayed
as if there were no Decalogue, no Sermon on the Mount, no
Gospel of redeeming love, and no responsibility of the human soul to the living God, it is good to have this account of
an American boyhood and young manhood nurtured in a
healthier climate than ours.

Although he was not a New Englander, Dr. Macartney's
home reflected the plain living and high thinking tradition-

ally associated with the New England of a former age. His was a family where high-mindedness and integrity were the everyday manifestation of the great truths of the Westminster Shorter Catechism. Filial devotion, honesty, decency, and industry shine through these pages. Such transparency of character and loftiness of purpose are precious elements of our American heritage. They go hand in hand with a depth of culture and a quiet joy far removed from the tension and unrest typical of the secularized home of today.

From the time in which Clarence Macartney came to maturity we are now separated by two World Wars and by the well-nigh incredible advances of modern science and technology. The problems facing us are of a difficulty and complexity scarcely dreamed of sixty years ago. But the great virtues do not change. This autobiography is an inspiring reminder that an authentic and living part of our American birthright lies in the kind of values—integrity, decency, high-mindedness, moral strength, purity of purpose, based upon an abiding faith in the Lord Jesus Christ according to the Scriptures—that made Clarence Edward Macartney the great minister he was.

It is fortunate that the publishers were able to enlist Dr. J. Clyde Henry as editor of the manuscript, which contained certain gaps that could be appropriately bridged only by someone intimately acquainted with Dr. Macartney and his work. Dr. Henry, who was associated with Dr. Macartney for twelve years in the ministry of the First Presbyterian Church of Pittsburgh, has accomplished the task admirably and unobtrusively. Moreover, the essay he has contributed gives a living picture of the man he knew so well.

FRANK GAEBELEIN

Stony Brook

INTRODUCTION

WHEN death claims a man who has been held in high admiration and affection, one begins fondly to embroider cherished memories so that the stark outline may be preserved in living colors. There is the temptation that the heart will give wings to rhapsodic utterance unshared by those to whom he was a stranger. But there is the danger, equally grave, that those who knew him only from afar may not know the inspiration and ideals that made the man.

William Cowper, in *The Task,* describes the character of the true minister:

> I would express him simple, grave, sincere;
> In doctrine uncorrupt; in language plain,
> And plain in manner; decent, solemn, chaste,
> And natural in gesture; much impress'd
> Himself, as conscious of his awful charge,
> And anxious mainly that the flock he feeds
> May feel it too; affectionate in look,
> And tender in address, as well becomes
> A messenger of grace to guilty men.

Clarence Edward Macartney could have sat for that portrait. He was such a messenger of grace.

Man is such a mystery to himself that it seems presumptuous to attempt to describe another's character. Like some unknown island which presents to the explorer only its shoreline, now rocky and forbidding, now pleasant and inviting, while the heartland is unrevealed, so is man. Yet, where its streams and fountains flow into the sea, there may be found, carried on its waters, evidences of an inner life easy to interpret and understand. And the soul of every man has such inlets where the heart is revealed.

One cannot begin to understand Dr. Macartney as a person until the unfailing springs of inspiration which flowed from his home are discovered. Dr. John Longfellow McCartney, his father, was a man of strong personality and extraordinarily wide general knowledge. The mother, however, by the unanimous testimony of the children, was the dominant personality in the home—a woman of high culture, wide learning, broad sympathies, and deep spirituality. Dr. Macartney described his home thus: ". . . a godly father and godly mother, working and praying for their Lord and their children, where no word of temper and no act of violence was ever heard or seen, and where the Christian life was not only taught out of Psalm Book and catechism, and Bible and commentary, but was itself drawn out in living and unforgettable characters of beauty and power which still shine as stars in heaven to comfort, guide and cheer us on our way."

In the pulpit Dr. Macartney studiously avoided personal references of an intimate nature, with one exception: he did not hesitate to refer to the influence of his home. He wrote, "The preacher always runs some risk when he uses his own personal experiences for illustrations. . . . There is no doubt that wisely selected illustrations from personal experience will often be very effective. If a man has had a godly home and godly parents, references to that home and to those parents will always be acceptable and timely."

The family expeditions along murmuring streams, over covered bridges, up pleasant glens, visiting neighboring farms, gave the boy a love for the countryside which a ministry of half a century in the heart of three cities never quenched. In later years he delighted to go with members of his staff or other friends to spread their table on some flat rock above a quiet stream, or on some green field with the beautiful countryside and its peaceful relaxation. Here, with the responsibilities of the church laid aside, he was a boy again, playing family games such as charades, or recalling early memories, or wandering through the woods. At summer camps the boys thrilled to his adventure stories, and loved to follow him on a hike over the hills when he would organize them into an army. Many men and women swore that never again would they start out with him on a Sunday afternoon stroll which led them up and down steep trails and cut through tangled underbrush, took them over fences and across streams, before they returned to their starting place.

He grew up on a college campus, and the pranks of the college students and the exploits of athletic teams brought spice to life whose flavor Dr. Macartney always enjoyed. His church staff learned to be suspicious of assignments on the first day of April, after several had gone to comfort the sick at non-existent addresses, or to arrange weddings for non-existent couples, or to deliver packages to non-scheduled trains. His interest in athletics, particularly baseball, continued to the very end. Many a boy was amazed to hear the learned preacher cite records and averages of players and teams, and listened with new respect when he spoke of spiritual things.

It was in the home that he preached his first sermons, with the family properly seated as the congregation. Sometimes his brother was called on to act out the dramatic Bible scene. He recalled the first two sermons he worked on as a mere child. The text of one was "Jesus wept," the text of the other, "There shall be weeping and wailing and gnashing of teeth." He then commented, "After all, the two texts and the two childish sermons were true to the Scripture and true to the Gospel, for the prophets, the apostles and Jesus himself strike these two notes: God's judgment and mercy, his compassion, and the penalty upon sin."

Dr. Macartney was always conscious of the dignity of the pastoral office. Professor Oswald T. Allis, a seminary classmate, said, "I recall one spring day near the end of our first year seeing two distinguished-looking gentlemen sallying forth from Hodge Hall on their way to preaching appointments on the following Sabbath day. Their black tail coats, high hats and patent leather shoes were such a contrast to the rather careless apparel ordinarily worn about the campus that I remember being quite impressed." The two were Clarence Macartney and his older brother, Albert. A picture of him during the days at Paterson shows a handsome young man with dark, wavy hair, clothed in a pulpit robe, wearing a black rabat and clerical collar—quite a contrast to the plain Covenanter dress he was accustomed to, and, I suppose, somewhat of an innovation for those days in Presbyterian circles. He was always particular about pulpit appearance, and deplored the wearing in the pulpit of "wall-paper neckties," as he called them, with splashes of bright colors. He enjoyed laughing with his assistants as they later recalled their early discomfiture when they were sent to purchase or exchange some article of apparel—necktie, shirt, or suit (for which the Doctor quite likely would pay)—so that they would make a more proper appearance behind the sacred desk.

There was nothing strikingly distinctive about his pastoral ministry, unless it was the fidelity with which he performed it. In a busy ministry with five regular preaching and speaking responsibilities each week, and frequently more, he called in the homes and in the hospitals three and four afternoons and two and three evenings every week. There was probably not a home in the widespread congregation in which he had not called and offered prayer. There are some who noticed only the external reserve of the man in public appearance. Yet it took but little association with him to discover the warm heart and sympathetic spirit which was the true person. He was as welcome, and as much at home, in the humble dwelling of the poor as he was in the house of affluence. The strata of society, and he ministered to them all, were a matter of indifference to him. He did not "talk down" to any; he did not seek to "live up to" any. Because he was primarily the minister of Jesus Christ, he was indifferent to the differences among men.

Those who were not altogether sympathetic with his stand, or who were unacquainted with the hidden springs of motivation, sometimes complained of his indifference to public opinion. A Pittsburgh magazine published a biographic sketch of him which was not enthusiastically complimentary. The writer said of Dr. Macartney: "His sermons against the secularization of the Sabbath, his condemnation of current motion pictures, liquor advertising, and vice conditions in the city, have time and again made newspaper stories. He never considers the popularity of his stands. Recently when he objected to a Sunday war bond rally the newspapers were deluged with critical letters suggesting that if America had lost the war she might have lost her churches. Firm in his convictions, he paid no attention."

But he was sensitive to the pulse of the city and the nation. Both in Philadelphia and Pittsburgh, he took midnight walks through the "tenderloin" section, and visited with the hapless men brought by the police in the middle of the night into the station houses. No one who was there will forget the services on D-Day and V-E Day conducted from the Geneva pulpit above the city street, when Sixth Avenue was thronged from corner to corner, as he led the people in the spontaneous expression of prayer and dedication. He was a true patriot, who delighted to remind his church and country of the blood-bought heritage of America, and the debt we owe to the heroes of the nation.

His preaching was always Bible-centered. Two days before he died, he said to his brother Robertson, who was leaving to preach in a nearby pulpit, "Put all the Bible you can into it." There is scarcely one familiar character of the Old or New Testament that was not the theme of some sermon, hardly a scene which he did not illuminate with his rare powers of description. A newspaper comment after his death mentioned "the imagery and matchless timing of his story-telling, like the glorious hues of a master's brush stroking the picture of life." Here all the treasures of intelligence, all the fountains of emotion, were brought into play. He dreamed dreams and saw visions, he communed with the spirits of just men made perfect, but in all he spoke to the hearts of men. He was frequently dramatic but never theatrical. The first impression one received from Dr. Macartney's preaching was its simplicity—a single theme stated, illustrated and applied, yet always binding the heart of man to the heart of the Gospel. He frequently used the great moral words—influence, opportunity, conscience, affection, repentance, and so forth. But he clothed them with living forms, marched them up the church aisles, and bade them testify for themselves.

All his preaching revolved around the "grand particularities of the faith." He insisted that without the historical foundation of revelation as an actual record of events, the Christian gospel has no power as a symbolic record of experience. His doctrines were not "fashion'd to the varying hour." Standing in the Reformed tradition, he took his position without mental reservation upon the Word of God as "the only infallible rule of faith and practice." He preached the truth of the Incarnation, based not upon metaphysical speculation, but upon the historical fact of the Virgin Birth. He preached often on the doctrine of immortality, basing his belief not on the moral necessity of such a hope, but upon the bodily resurrection of Jesus Christ. And in the light of these two doctrines he lifted high the cross of Christ in all its shame and all its glory: "No one who has knelt as a penitent sinner at the foot of the cross will find anything in the 'fountain filled with blood' to offend him, but much to thrill him." Then followed those other great themes of the Christian revelation: the sovereignty of God, His providence in personal life, and the grand and awful message of the final judgment and eternal redemption.

His ministry covered the period of religious controversy when some were preaching "another gospel which is not another," using dishonest semantics to emasculate words of historic Biblical and redemptive meaning. Dr. Macartney did not hesitate to enter the lists and to raise his standard. He was not a contentious man, but he was conscientious. He attacked the unconscious or unconfessed unitarianism which had crept into the Church as an enemy of Christ and of the Gospel. Against the immorality of infidelity and the cowardice of compromise within the Church, he called for a straightforward allegiance to the Confessional standards, and to the plain statements of the historic creeds. He recognized that the Church cannot be built upon the shifting sands of reason nor upon the quicksands of feeling, but only upon the facts of objective revelation. Those within the Church who were tolerant of unbelief raised a counter-protest on the pretense of safeguarding the unity and liberty of the Church, straining at a gnat of supposed ecclesiastical irregularity while they gulped down without effort a whole camel of theological irregularity. They called for liberty to believe what they pleased, while vowing their acceptance of and loyalty to the Confession of Faith. This is simply anarchy founded upon unreality and dishonesty. To Dr. Macartney this historic debate was no mere academic matter. (And there is indeed a moral fault running through the character of the preacher in the Confessional church who cannot repeat the Apostles' Creed without lying, and the church which tolerates such a preacher is in spiritual peril.) A Pittsburgh newspaper editorial said of Dr. Macartney: "In an age of confusion and fear, the stalwart minister of First Church has stood like a veritable Gibraltar for the fundamental doctrines of the Christian faith." He received his share of abuse, but without bitterness. There is an ungodly conceit which enthrones reason, and will not accept anything the reason does not approve. And there is a godly conceit which enthrones Christ and his Word, and will not receive anything which is contrary to them. When Dr. Macartney was installed as pastor in Pittsburgh, the church received a letter from Dr. Francis L. Patton, in which the noted theologian said: "The new minister of your church will come with a message and not a query, and will be fully conscious that zeal in the pulpit will never grow out of doubt in the study."

Dr. Macartney's preaching was essentially evangelistic. He spoke with the shepherd's heart, and in practically every sermon he pointed out the way of salvation. On one occasion I was asked to make a selection of Dr. Macartney's printed sermons for a missionary who wanted to translate them to use in his program of radio evangelism. I was struck by the fact, as I reviewed the sermons, that practically all of them, except those preached on special themes, with but little adaptation were suitable. During the war years, bundles of the printed sermons were sent to chaplains all over the world. Many service men wrote to testify that they had been brought, or brought back, to Christian faith by reading the sermons. Homer Rodeheaver said to me after a service at which Dr. Macartney preached: "I told him once that, if he would devote all his time to it, he could be the greatest evangelist of this century."

At the service celebrating the twenty-fifth anniversary of the Doctor's pastorate in Pittsburgh, Dr. Frederick W. Loetscher, who had been on the faculty at Princeton Seminary when Dr. Macartney was a student, was invited to preach. In his introductory remarks Dr. Loetscher said, speaking of Dr. Macartney the preacher:

> "Of course, there is always something elusive about the secret of so conspicuous success, but some facts are obvious to us all. Even the casual observer must be impressed by this sturdy, dignified, intensely earnest personality, by that vibrant, well-controlled voice that can fill any auditorium and express any kind of emotion, by those abundant intellectual resources that betoken not only an intimate acquaintance with the Word of God but wide reading along collateral lines of study and in many a choice field of general literature. Then, too, one must take note of that admirable diction, so natural, so fresh, so vital, and of the clear, graceful, colorful style. Evidently knowledge is here wedded to a nimble fancy and a vigorous imagination. But all this would

not explain the extraordinary effectiveness of this preacher's spoken and written word. No, that power is essentially moral and spiritual."

The church historian then preached, with his accustomed eloquence, on Barnabas, using as his text, "For he was a good man, and full of the Holy Spirit and of faith." At the conclusion of his sermon he said:

"My friends, I am sure that all who know the life and work of the pastor of this church would have no hesitation in saying that he is quite as worthy of the notable tribute of this text as was the original recipient of it. And when I think of his ministrations in this pulpit I feel that one might fittingly appraise them by saying that he has done ample justice to the two meanings of this name Barnabas, 'Son of Exhortation,' 'Son of Consolation.' Year after year he has been admonishing multitudes of hearers and readers of his sermons, probing their hearts and consciences and warning them against the tragic consequences of unforgiven sin, yet never forgetting the sweetness of the evangel, the wonder of redeeming grace, the comfort, the peace, the joy of the soul that has been quickened by the Holy Spirit unto 'repentance toward God and faith in the Lord Jesus Christ.' With endless variety of texts and topics, with a never failing vigor and freshness of treatment, he has been applying biblical truth to all kinds of religious and moral issues, and every kind of human relationship and human need; but his primary aim, I am sure, has always been to make known how the Word of God, now in one way and now in another, answers these two all-comprehending questions, What is the good life? and How is it to be attained? And so well has he done this that I am sure many of us will now add in our tribute to him that last clause in the verse from which this text is taken, that brightest gem in the crown of the faithful minister of the gospel: 'and much people was added unto the Lord.' "

The writing of this autobiography was evidently begun during the year when Dr. Macartney was out of his pulpit because of illness. In June, 1948, Dr. Macartney entered the hospital for treatment of a condition which had annoyed and weakened him for some months. What he had anticipated as a few weeks at the most actually became a prolonged hospital experience with three major surgical operations and months of recuperation. It was not until May of the following year that he was able to return to his pulpit. The topic of his first sermon when he came back was "I Went Into Arabia," from the text in Galatians. He made no allusion to his recent illness, but it was evident to all that the sermon had been suggested by his own experience. He spoke of how we are lifted from time to time out of our accustomed place and work in life, and set aside for a period, as St. Paul was, in a place of retirement, solitude and meditation; and how in such experiences there are great blessings, and how God speaks a word then that he may not speak at any other time.

After this, Dr. Macartney began to spend more and more of his vacation periods at Fern Cliffe, the boyhood home which still occupies its prominent place on the campus of Geneva College. The house had been used by the college for some years as the president's home, and then briefly as a girls' dormitory. It had only the usual dormitory furniture in it, but Dr. Macartney loved to invite friends to visit him there, and with great pride entertained his guests, unmindful of the limited facilities. At his twenty-fifth anniversary as pastor in Pittsburgh, the First Church—with the permission of the college, which had given him full use of the house—furnished the first floor of Fern Cliffe and part of the second. He did not know what had been done, and when, in company with his brothers and sister who came for the celebration, he first saw the old home restored to its loveliness and comfort, he was moved almost too deeply for utterance.

In September, 1953, after a ministry of twenty-six and a half years in Pittsburgh, which attracted throngs every Sunday morning and evening, and after contending for five years with the handicap of illness, he retired to spend his last days at Fern Cliffe. He fulfilled the dream of Goldsmith's Wanderer:

> In all my wanderings round this world of care,
> In all my griefs—and God has giv'n my share,
> I still had hopes my latest hours to crown,
> Amidst these humble bow'rs to lay me down,
> To husband out life's taper at the close,
> And keep the flame from wasting by repose.
> Around my feet an evening group to draw,
> And tell of all I felt and all I saw;
> And as a hare whom hounds and horns pursue,
> Pants to the place from whence at first he flew,
> I still had hopes, my long vexations past,
> Here to return—and die at Home at last.

Dr. Macartney continued preaching and writing for more than two and a half years until increasing illness halted his steps and at last confined him to bed. During his later

ministry he had written several hymns, many of which had
been sung by the congregation. One of these, The Trial of
Job, concluded with a prayer that was answered.

O God, like Job, grant me the faith to hold
To Thee, though all I have and love should fall;
To see Thy Face, to hear Thy loving call;
And from Thy furnace I'll come forth as gold.

On the last visits I had with him, one in the hospital and
one at home, he asked me to read from the book of Job.
"Read the part where it says 'Shall we receive good at the
hand of the Lord and shall we not receive evil?' " And again,
"Read that part 'In all this Job sinned not, nor charged God
foolishly.' " With members of the family who came to spend
the last vigil with him, he revived the custom of family
prayers, and once again the home was filled with the music
of the Psalter. His mind remained active to the end—pre-
paring sermons and manuscripts for publication, with special
concern at the very last for the autobiography. Knowing that
death drew nigh, he planned his funeral service to be a
simple testimony of praise to Jesus Christ and his triumphant
grace. He chose the hymns "Rock of Ages," "The Twenty-
third Psalm" and "Amazing Grace" as a witness to his faith.
His last message to his friends was, "Tell them my anchor
still holds." Then in the evening on February 19, 1957, he
closed his eyes in sleep and put on immortality.

In summing up the life of John Bunyan, Dr. Macartney
wrote, "The bell which Bunyan struck three centuries ago,
high up on the tower of his allegory, still vibrates with its
ancient melody, ever haunting the imagination of mankind,
its tones as deep and sweet and true as ever, for they echo
the deep eternal truths of sin, atonement, redemption, re-

generation, judgment to come, and life everlasting." These words are descriptive of the life and ministry of Dr. Macartney. He was a faithful minister of the Incarnate God, a messenger of redeeming grace.

CHAPTER I

IN THE BEGINNING

WHEN Nebuchadnezzar brought his Medean bride to Babylon, he built for her the celebrated Hanging Gardens in order that Amytis, brought up in the hill country, might not feel homesick and depressed in the flat plains of the Euphrates. I was born on a hilltop for the same reason: moved by the same tender consideration, my father—when he brought his bride from her beautiful home on the Cathgen Braes in Scotland to Northwood in Logan County, Ohio, where the land begins to flatten out into the Mississippi valley—built his home for her on the only hill in the vicinity. It was there, in that pleasantly located cottage, on a September day, when the hickory, elm, and maple trees in the forests about Northwood were turning yellow pale and hectic red, and the fields were strewn with the blue asters and the goldenrod, that I began my earthly pilgrimage and warfare.

I was the last in a family of seven children—three sisters and four brothers. Of the three sisters, only one was living when I arrived, but through my mother's frequent mention of the other two, they became in time quite real to me. Born thus in a Protestant minister's home, I had, according to the authorities in heredity and environment, and according to

27

the record of *Who's Who,* a distinct advantage in the manner and circumstance of my entering life. Like the great majority of ministers' sons, I was born into a home of plain living and high thinking.

My father, who married rather late in life, was, at the time of my birth, fifty-one years old. The Macartneys, spelled also McCartney, came to America in the first years of the nineteenth century from County Antrim in Ireland. When travelling once through that part of Ireland, I found the Macartneys were still numerous there. Some who had borne the name in the past had achieved considerable distinction in British government circles, and some today carry high titles. I was on my way one day to visit one of the latter at his seat, but happening to call at the home of a Presbyterian minister, I was informed that this particular Macartney was generally drunk, and so gave up the visit.

It must have been quite a group of Macartneys who came from County Antrim in Ireland to County Guernsey in Ohio about 1800. Among them were two brothers, William, my grandfather, and John, a man who rose to considerable affluence and prominence in Guernsey County. They were the sons of Henry and Jane Strong McCartney. These brothers, and those with them, hewed out for themselves homes and farms in the wilderness, some ten miles out from what is now Cambridge, the County seat. On a pilgrimage through that district I was not able to locate the site of my grandfather's homestead, save to learn that it was in the vicinity of Sugar Tree, Salem Church, and Kimbolton.

From farming the family branched out into road building and later into railroad building. They were contractors on the famous National Pike or Cumberland Road, from Baltimore to St. Louis, later known as Highway 40. Driving through Ohio on Number 40, one notes the exceedingly graceful "S" bridges. They are not adapted for automobile

28

traffic because of their winding shape, but fortunately a few of them have been preserved and can be seen hard by the modern concrete bridges. The story goes that the architect and engineer for the "S" bridges was an Englishman, Benjamin H. Latrobe. Latrobe stopped at the McCartney's Inn, near the creek, and John McCartney, who was also a stone mason, solicited the contract. When the engineer sneeringly suggested that he could not carry out so difficult a design, McCartney replied that he could build any bridge "that any d---- Englishman could plan." He was accorded the contract, and the work was completed in 1828, and in these beautiful and picturesque bridges he built an abiding monument to himself. And when we come to think of it, what better monument could a man leave behind him than a good bridge? Once on a journey through Scotland I happened to look out of the window at the station where the train stopped, and saw the name Auldgarth. This brought back to me Thomas Carlyle and his beautiful tribute in the *Reminiscences* to his stone-mason father, James Carlyle, who helped to build that bridge at Auldgarth:

> "A noble craft is that of a mason: a good building will last longer than most books, than one book of a million. The Auldgarth bridge still spans the water silently, defies its chafing. There hangs it, and will hang, grim and strong, when of all the cunning hands that piled it together, perhaps the last now is powerless in the sleep of death. O Time! O Time! wondrous and fearful art thou; yet there is in man what is above thee."

Latrobe was so pleased with the work in Ohio that he took McCartney to Maryland. There John McCartney, who was my great-uncle, was contracted to build the Thomas Viaduct, bridging the Patapsco River at Relay, Maryland. Termed one of the most beautiful stone viaducts in the United States, it was completed in 1835, and still carries the trains from the West into Baltimore. According to the family record, I ought to have been a builder and engineer, for not only had I back of me these road builders and bridge builders, but also, on my mother's side, was connected with Henry Bell, who in Scotland ranks as one of the inventors of the steamship. But it was appointed of old that in a humble capacity I should be an engineer on the Way of Life.

In 1840 Guernsey County was frontier territory. My father told me how he learned to swim when, after a fight with an Indian with whom he was crossing a stream, the canoe was overturned, and it was a case of sink or swim. He used to tell us, too, how they sometimes could see a bear and her cubs sunning themselves on a big rock near the farm. One winter day a neighbor was driving his bobsled home from the market. As he sat dozing on his seat while passing through a woods, the oxen suddenly began to snort in terror and bolted for home. The farmer looked around to see what the trouble was, and saw that a big bear had boarded the sled, whereupon the frightened man rolled from his seat into the snow. When the oxen finally reached home they ran into the barn. There the bear disembarked and climbed to a beam under the roof of the barn, where he was shot. Another tale Father told us was how their mongrel dog, Brave, when a bull or steer became rambunctious, would run in under the bull's belly, sink his teeth into the bull's sensitive nose, then brace himself and pull back with that wonderful strength of a dog's jaws and shoulders, and throw the bull on his back.

My grandfather died in 1833, when he was only forty-two years of age. On my search for the family homestead I saw near the highway in the country near North Salem, Ohio, a number of pine trees and under them several graves. I said to my brother who was with me, "Perhaps this is the place where our grandfather is buried." And sure enough, it was. There, row upon row, slept the Macartneys, the Bells, and the Martins, all related and all builders of the civilization of that part of Ohio. My grandmother was left with the care of three daughters and five sons. In order that she might be relieved somewhat of her burden, the two youngest sons, John, my father, and James, were taken to the home of my father's Uncle Henry. (Some time after my grandfather's death, my grandmother married the Reverend Robert Wallace, a Reformed Presbyterian minister, and the pioneer missionary of the Covenanter Church in Ohio.) Henry Macartney's commodious frame house is still standing, and near it his first home, an unusually large log cabin. It must have been to this cabin that my father and uncle were taken after their father's death. We have the memory of Father telling us of how in the winter evenings he would lift a board in the floor of the cabin and bring up nuts and apples which they would eat about the fire. In the cabin there was and is an enormous fireplace. I still hope some day to get that fireplace and rebuild it in a home of my own.

I never heard my father speak of his early schooling. No doubt he attended one of the district schools and read his lessons out of that treasury of good literature and good morals— *McGuffey's Readers*—which appeared in the 1830's, and attained through the years an extraordinary circulation of thirty million copies. William McGuffey was born near Claysville in Washington County, Pennsylvania, but as a child was brought up on the Connecticut Preserve near Youngstown, Ohio. One night a Presbyterian minister, Thomas Hughes, happened to hear McGuffey's mother praying for her son, that a way might be opened for his education. Hughes took the young McGuffey into the old Stone Academy at Greersburg, now Darlington, Pennsylvania. From the

Academy he went to Washington College, now Washington and Jefferson. He was licensed but never ordained as a Presbyterian minister. After teaching for a time, he became president of Cincinnati University, and then of Ohio University at Athens. He ended his illustratious career as Professor of Moral Philosophy at the University of Virginia. *McGuffey's Readers* did more to inculcate Christian morality and pitch the standards of literary taste in America than any other book save the Bible.

The Macartneys, first in Ireland and then in Ohio, were of the Reformed Presbyterian persuasion, and in that splendid training school of psalm-singing, oath-refusing, secret-society abominating, non-voting and Bible-believing Covenanters, my father was "brought up in the nurture and admonition of the Lord." It was, I think, the Salem Church where they worshiped. My father and his younger brother, James, used to walk ten miles, summer and winter, to that wilderness house of worship, where they sat out the twenty-minute "Long" prayer, a thirty-minute "explanation" of the Psalm, and a one-hour sermon. Today we have put the clock on public worship. People sit all afternoon at a baseball or football game, or for three hours at a theatre, and think not of the clock. But now, if the whole church service exceeds one hour, there is restlessness and discontent. What would happen today to people who walked ten miles each way to church? I suppose they would be in need of a stretcher.

I do not recall having heard my father say where or how he prepared for college; but in 1851 he was graduated from Jefferson College at Canonsburg, Pennsylvania. Jefferson, now Washington and Jefferson, was at that time one of the first centers of learning west of the Allegheny Mountains, and vied in numbers and prestige with some of the older colleges of the East. The founder of Jefferson was the renowned John McMillan, the Princeton-trained minister who crossed the mountains with his bride in 1775 and became pastor of the Chartiers Creek Presbyterian Church, also known as the Hill Church, not far from Canonsburg, and where, almost a century later, Woodrow Wilson's father was the pastor.

Looking to the future of the Church and the ministry, McMillan took six young men into his home to train them for the ministry. Later, a log cabin schoolhouse was built adjoining his manse. In 1794, the Academy was established at Canonsburg, and in time became Jefferson College. The log cabin where it started may now be seen at Canonsburg in front of Providence Hall, one of the original buildings of the college, but now the Junior High School. Jefferson held high repute in the South and, until the Civil War, many of the students were from that section. Among those who were in college at the same time as my father were: Senator Matthew Stanley Quay, 1850, the President-Maker, justly termed "the Napoleon of Politics"; Benjamin H. Bristow, 1851, Grant's Secretary of the Treasury, who prosecuted the Whiskey Ring; Andrew Hepburn, President of the University of Ohio; Bishop William Edward McLaren, 1851, of Illinois; James Woodrow, Woodrow Wilson's uncle; Albert Johnson, killed in the Sepoy Mutiny; Matthew Brown Riddle, 1852, noted New Testament scholar; and William Mitchell, 1853, Justice of the Supreme Court of Minnesota and father of William D. Mitchell, Attorney General under Hoover.

The president of Jefferson College at that time was the Reverend Alexander B. Brown. Driving recently through New Concord, Ohio, I saw a tablet on a plain house on the main street, telling that in that house was born William Rainey Harper, the first president of the University of Chicago. Dr. Harper's father was a student at nearby Washington College during my father's days at Jefferson, and I remember Father telling me how, after the long "Senior vacation," he and Harper, with two young ladies, drove all the way from New Concord to Canonsburg for his Commencement.

After my father's graduation at Jefferson, he became principal of the Academy of West Carlisle, Ohio. In 1852 he was editor of the *Literary Cabinet* published at Zanesville, Ohio, and in 1854 became principal of the high school of that city. He was elected Professor of Mathematics in 1855, at the recently established Muskingum College, now at New Concord, Ohio. In 1856, my father entered the theological seminary of the Reformed Presbyterian Church at Allegheny City, Pennsylvania. Either during his seminary term or between college and seminary, he must have spent some time in business, for he used to tell us how he had cleared several hundred dollars in gold, selling maps. This was during the exciting days of "Bleeding Kansas" and the fierce debates over slavery. At a public meeting in St. Louis, Father gave fearless expression to his abolitionist sentiments, and was either put out of the hall, or invited to leave the city. As a young man in Ohio he worked on the Underground Railroad. One of his stirring stories was how on a cold winter's night he carried a Negro babe in his arms, helping the mother on to the next "station." It is a somewhat curious and interesting fact that the most fearless and outspoken enemies of slavery were, at the one extreme, the ministers of the Covenanter Church, the most rigidly orthodox of all the churches, and at the other extreme, those of the Unitarian Church, the most liberal of all the churches, and by the Covenanters regarded not as a church at all, but rather as a "synagogue of Satan."

CHAPTER II

MY MOTHER

IN 1858, Father went abroad to study theology in Glasgow. While there he received an invitation to go down to Rothesay on the Isle of Bute, where he preached in the Reformed Presbyterian Church. When he went into the pulpit he saw sitting in the front gallery pew John Robertson, a successful cotton-mill owner, and his family. The face among the seven children which held his attention was that of the eldest daughter, Catherine. The young minister was invited to dine with the family after the service, where he saw more of Catherine. A few days afterwards, he went to a picnic at the beautiful family home at Blairbeth. As he was pushing Catherine in a swing something broke and she fell from the swing, her hoop skirts coming up about her head. The young theolog extricated her from this difficulty, at the same time discreetly looking in the other direction.

When Father looked down from the pulpit that Sabbath morning at Rothesay and saw Catherine in the pew, he was looking into the face of his wife, into the face of his seven children, into the face of destiny. My mother's family was of Scottish and French Huguenot blood. One of my Christian names, but rarely used, is Noble. The Nobles were Hugue-

nots and cloth-manufacturers in France, who settled in Rothesay because of some qualities in the water there which were
favorable to dyeing. Covenanter and Huguenot—that makes
a strain hard to surpass. One of the Nobles' daughters married a Young, and of this marriage came my grandmother on
my mother's side. A large portrait of her in her widow's cap
used to hang over the mantelpiece in our living room at home.
I was looking at it recently on the wall of my sister's home at
Stanford University. The portrait shows her a woman of
strong, honest, thrifty, cautious character.

A Mr. Doig, operator of a cotton mill at Rothesay, had
died, and his widow asked her minister in the church at Paisley if he knew of anyone he could recommend as manager of
the mill. The minister said he knew the very man for the
post and named young John Robertson, my grandfather. The
young couple went down to Rothesay, where my grandfather
took charge of the little mill. At first they lived in a humble
cottage near the mill, but as the business prospered they removed with their children to Hillhead, a fine home on the
hill above the town looking over Rothesay and the Clyde.
How often I have heard my mother speak of her early days
on the lovely Isle of Bute; the view of the mountains of Arran
from her window; the church where she worshipped; her first
teacher; the Atlantic liners bound for America, and the
steamers coming down from Glasgow and Greenock; the
fishermen calling their fish in the streets when a catch of
herring came in; her family singing at family worship: "O
God of Bethel" or "Beethel," as her father pronounced it;
the excursions to Ettrick Bay, and racing her pony along the
sands. Mother had a deep vein of sentiment and romanticism
in her, and no doubt her early years in lovely Bute had something to do with that. In 1914 my brother Albert and I had
the joy of visiting Rothesay with Mother and the youngest of
her brothers, Joseph. We sat by her side on the Sabbath in

the church, and thought of that first meeting at Rothesay in the long ago when my father looked down from the pulpit and saw the face of Catherine Robertson in the pew before him. This time it was not only a Sabbath of tender memories of the past but one of stirring contemporary events, for as the congregation came out from the church on that August Sabbath, we heard them talking of the battles in which Rothesay soldiers were fighting with the Expeditionary Force in France in World War I.

The courtship of my father and mother was a long one— ten years—and not altogether smooth, chiefly perhaps because of distance. My grandfather had prospered greatly in his new mill, the Newhall Factory at Bridgeton on the outskirts of Glasgow, and had purchased a handsome estate on the Cathgen Braes. In time his mill became the largest cotton factory in the world. My grandfather, deeply attached to his favorite daughter, could not bear to think of her marrying a poor American preacher and leaving Blairbeth to go across the sea to a little backwoods hamlet in Ohio, where my father had become the minister of the First Miami congregation at Northwood. Two of my mother's brothers had been sent to America to spy out the land at Northwood. When they returned they reported that it would never do for the daughter of John Robertson to go from her beautiful home to live in such a place. So for years the battle raged to and fro. At length, like Rebecca of old when asked if she would go to become the bride of Isaac, "Wilt thou go with this man?", Mother said firmly and finally, "I will go." They were married at Blairbeth, my mother's home, on a beautiful August day in 1868.

At the last moment my grandfather, seated in his office at the mill on the day of the wedding, at the entreaty of an old friend, relented and made his appearance at the marriage. The ceremony was performed by a friend of my father, the

Reverend William Pollock Johnston, a young minister from Ohio, who was travelling in Scotland at the time. He was later president of Geneva College. Forty-seven years afterwards the same Dr. Johnston officiated at the marriage of my brother Albert in Chicago. He also had a part in the marriage of my sister Wilhelmina to Dr. Albert L. Guerard of Stanford University.

When the train carrying the bride and groom to Liverpool to board the steamer for New York crossed the border near Carlisle my father, in exultation that his ten-year siege and campaign had come to a victorious conclusion, let down the window in the compartment, waved his beaver in the air, and let out a shout of triumphant joy. That was the most emotional thing I ever heard of my father doing.

"A remarkable woman!" How often in coming across persons who knew my mother have I heard that exclamation on their lips. A remarkable woman indeed: remarkable in strength of intellect, in deep interest in the lives of others; remarkable in her tender affection for her children; remarkable in her appreciation of good literature; remarkable for her daily intercessions for her family at the Throne of Grace; and remarkable for her unflagging zeal and devotion to her Redeemer's Kingdom. Her family were members of the Great Hamilton Street Reformed Presbyterian Church in Glasgow, of which Dr. John Symington was the minister. Often I heard Mother speak of a sermon preached by Dr. Symington on the text, "Occupy Till I Come." John G. Paton, afterwards the famous missionary to the New Hebrides, was the city missionary for Mother's church. He once came to visit us at our home in Beaver Falls, and I remember well his long white patriarchal beard and the benediction of his countenance. When driving in the family carriage from Blairbeth to Glasgow and passing through Rutherglen where her father's mill was, Mother would frequently see a pale face pressed against the window high up in one of the tenements. One day she had the coachman stop the carriage and, alighting, made her way through the "close" and up the dark winding stairway to the chamber where she had seen the face at the window. There she found a frail, crippled girl. After that visit Mother started a Friday-night Bible class for mill girls. The class grew rapidly in numbers and became a means of blessing to hundreds of the mill girls and women. I have in my library Thomson's *The Land and the Book,* still one of the best works on the Holy Land, which was presented to Mother on her wedding day by her Friday-night class. It bears this inscription: "To Catherine Robertson on her wedding day. 'Let us not be weary in well doing: for in due season we shall reap, if we faint not.'" Yes, Mother, thou hast reaped well indeed. Sometimes thou didst sow in tears, but ever thou didst come again with rejoicing, bringing thy sheaves with thee: sheaves from Rutherglen and Glasgow; sheaves from Northwood and Beaver Falls; sheaves from the generations of Geneva College students; sheaves from thine own family, for thy children today rise up and call thee blessed. Not empty-handed didst thou go to the King's Gate.

CHAPTER III

NORTHWOOD

ON their arrival at New York, Father and Mother spent the first few days at the Fifth Avenue Hotel. It was still standing when I began my ministry at Paterson, New Jersey, and was famous for its "Amen Corner," the corner in the lounge where New York's Republican boss, Thomas C. Platt, met with his lieutenants to plan the strategy of political campaigns. Whenever I went into the hotel, I recalled how shocked Mother was when, in the stately dining room, she saw well-dressed men and women holding ears of corn to their mouths, as they ate that most delightful fruit of the late summer fields. "Have I come," she asked herself, "to a land of barbarians?"

From the expensive Fifth Avenue Hotel they went to the home of Dr. J. R. Sloane, minister of the Covenanter Church on Twenty-third Street. Dr. Sloane was one of the first presidents of Geneva College, and one of the most eloquent of the abolitionists. At the time of the Draft Riots, in 1863, the mob came storming into his house. Dr. William Milligan Sloane, long-time professor at Columbia University, and author of the popular life of Napoleon, was the son of the Dr. Sloane at whose New York home Father and Mother were guests when they arrived in New York.

After a long and hot journey over the Baltimore & Ohio Railroad, Father and Mother reached Belle Center, Ohio, and then were driven to Northwood, the tiny hamlet where Father was pastor of the Covenanter Church, and where Geneva College, founded twenty years before, was located. The humble home on the hill, Elmwood Cottage, the unpaved streets, the uncultivated manners of the people, the lack of servants—all this made Northwood a tremendous contrast to the beautiful and well-appointed home at Blairbeth in Scotland.

At first Mother would hardly consent to have her boxes brought up from Belle Center and opened, for it seemed not quite possible to her that this crude frontier village was now to be her home. But courage, faith, and love won the battle. She took up her duties and her place in Elmwood Cottage, in the congregation, and in the college, and began to write the beautiful twelve-year chapter of her life at Northwood. There five of her children were born; there she experienced her first real struggles in life; there she entered into the joys and sorrows of the folk of the village; and there she drank her first deep cup of woe. It was on this wise: Mother's first-born child was a daughter, Therina. When she was three years old, Mother took her and the next child, Ernest, on a visit to her parents in Scotland. The grandparents were so fond of Therina that they asked Mother to leave her with them that winter, promising to come out themselves in the springtime and bring Therina with them. To this Mother consented, and sailed for America with Ernest. She never saw her daughter again. One cold March day Father came in from the post office, bringing with him one of the always-eagerly-awaited blue envelopes from Scotland. It was from her father, and commenced, "Our dear wee pet is no more." The child had taken scarlet fever and, after a brief illness, was gone. Thus Mother entered into the Valley of the Shadow.

It was a terrible blow, and for a time the bottom dropped out of life for her. Her diary of those days shows how dreadful a cup it was she had to drink. One excerpt reads: "Her hair! Oh, is this all of my child? My beautiful child? Is this the hair I used to curl, coaxing her to keep still? Oh, the little curly head! Where, where art thou, my Therina? Oh, Lord, I believe Thou hast taken her to Thyself! She is 'well and happy' with Thee. Help mine unbelief." Later she wrote: "Oh for strong undoubting faith! Oh, for patient, cheerful resignation! What times of doubt, infidelity I have had; of saying, 'But is there after all a God?' 'Is there after all a life hereafter?' Lord, thou art my God. Forgive my unworthy thoughts of Thee. Deliver me from the Enemy who plies me hard with infidel arguments. Oh, come, Holy Spirit, into my heart, and so take up thine abode there, and so make Thy presence to be known and felt there that there will be no room for doubting or questioning." So, in the end, faith and love were triumphant, and she once more took up the broken threads of life.

Long after, when I was a child, I used to see Mother stand before the large portrait of Therina which hung in the living room of our house at Beaver Falls, and, looking wistfully into the beautiful child's face, exclaim, "My wee Therina, where are you now!" That was the first time that I heard any discussion of the subject of recognition in the life to come. Mother used to wonder how she would recognize Therina in the heavenly life. Would she still be a child as she had known her? So Constance, in Shakespeare's *King John*, was fearful lest, when she met the imprisoned Prince Arthur, her son, in the life to come, she would not know him.

I have always felt that that great sorrow was a ministering angel to my mother and that the trial through which she passed, accepted by her as no accident or chance of fate but appointed of God for some good and wise end, enriched and strengthened her and fitted her to become a blessing to others. She used to quote to her children the words of God to Abraham: "Be thou a blessing." In Mother's diary for the day after she received the word that her daughter was dead is this entry: "Today I called on Miss Wylie, who seemed to be dying." Thus through her own great sorrow Mother took captivity captive, and in the fifty years that followed, until her death, brought a blessing into hundreds of lives.

In *Margaret Ogilvy,* James M. Barrie pays a beautiful tribute to his mother. In the chapter, "How My Mother Got Her Soft Face," he tells of his older brother, and his mother's ambition for his future distinction. When this son was thirteen, and away at school, the word came that he was very ill. The whole family trooped down the brae to the wooden station to see the mother off on her journey to get between death and her boy. Her ticket was taken and she had bidden her family goodbye when the father came out of the telegraph office and said huskily, "He's gone!" Barrie writes, "I knew my mother forever now." When she got home the first thing she expressed a wish to see was the christening robe, and she looked long at it, and then turned her face to the wall. "That is how she got her soft face, and her pathetic ways and her large charity, and why other mothers ran to her when they had lost a child. 'Dinna greet, poor Janet,' she would say to them; and they would answer, 'Ah, Margaret, but you're greeting yourself.' " Whenever I read that beautiful passage from *Margaret Ogilvy,* I think of my own mother, and how she too, in that great sorrow when her first-born died in far-off Scotland, "got her soft face and her pathetic ways and her large charity, and why other mothers ran to her when they had lost a child."

Geneva College, founded by a group of earnest, God-fearing Covenanters, opened its doors in 1848. It was founded by the Reformed Presbytery of the Lakes but shortly became independent of ecclesiastical control, although most of its fiscal board were of the Covenanter Church. In the notice sent abroad, before the opening of the college, its purpose was thus set forth: "A literary Institution upon Scriptural principles, making the Bible, with a selection of the best Christian authors in the Latin and Greek languages, as the textbook." This circular, too, made great claims for the location of the college. The site was described as "elevated, commanding an extensive view of the valley of the Miami, and of the surrounding beautiful and undulating country. . . . It is within some 30 minutes' walk of the Mad River and Lake Erie Railroad. The Columbus and Indianapolis Railroad, which will connect with the Philadelphia and Pittsburg, and with the Baltimore and Ohio rail roads, will cross the former railroad at Bellefontaine, near 'Geneva Hall,' thus affording facilities for ready conveyance from every part of the Union." As a matter of fact, however, Northwood was just a frontier hamlet in the midst of a clearing in the forest. When my two future uncles came out from Scotland to spy out the land and see if it were a fit habitation for their sister, one of them in his letters to Scotland, describing the road to Northwood, drew a sketch of his brother in front of him, with one foot and leg up to the hilt in mud, bending down and trying with both hands to extricate himself from the morass.

Yet, notwithstanding these primitive conditions, the little brick college at Northwood became in time a center of light and learning. Its "line is gone out through all the earth" and its "words to the end of the world." When in 1924, as Moderator of the General Assembly of the Presbyterian Church, U.S.A., I travelled through the country, there was hardly a service at which I preached, or a meeting at which I spoke, where some person from little Northwood did not come forward to tell me that he had known my father and mother. The village of Northwood was a prominent "station" on the Underground Railroad, and after the Civil War there were always freedmen in the student body.

The Civil War, with the consequent departure of the students, all but wrecked the college. In 1862, the Sheriff of Logan County sold it under the hammer to the highest bidder; but in 1864 five friends of the institution, one of whom was my father, subscribed a sum of money and bought the college back. Largely through the plea of my father, the Synod of the Covenanter Church was persuaded to take over the college, and its future was secure. About that time my father was placed in temporary charge of the college, and not long afterward was made Professor of Natural Science. A new era opened for the institution with the election of Dr. Henry H. George in 1872 as president. In that year one hundred and twenty-four students came from far and near to attend the classes. Not many years before, Yale had four hundred seventy-three students, Union three hundred, Columbia one hundred thirty, and Jefferson one hundred eighty-two. Little Geneva was thus not far behind in the academic procession.

CHAPTER IV

BEAVER FALLS

IN order that the college might be near the center of its Covenanter constituency, it was removed to Beaver Falls, Pennsylvania. In that thriving manufacturing town on the Beaver River, thirty miles north of Pittsburgh, the college was located on a ten-acre plot of ground given by the Economite Society. The Economites were a company of Christian Communists who had come from Bavaria in 1803-04 under the leadership of Georg Rapp, and settled first at Harmony in Butler County, Pennsylvania. Later they removed to the banks of the Wabash in Indiana, where they cleared the wilderness and built their new community, also called Harmony. In 1824 the Economites sold their buildings and land to Robert Owen, the Scottish socialist, who renamed it New Harmony. The followers of Rapp returned to Pennsylvania and settled in Beaver County on the Ohio River, naming their new home Economy, which is now part of Ambridge. The Economites held all things in common, waited for the imminent Second Coming of Christ, and abjured marriage. It was this latter doctrine, of course, which doomed them to ultimate extinction; but while they flourished they played a great part in the development of the Ohio valley.

They operated at the lower end of Beaver Falls what was at one time the largest cutlery in the world. Chinese coolies were imported as workmen. The Chinese were long gone when I came to boyhood, but the bones of their dead were still there, and several times when passing through the Chinese cemetery at the north end of Beaver Falls, I whistled to keep up my courage lest a ghost of one of these celestials should arise from his grave. True to their hoary custom of reverence for the dead and for their ancestors, the relatives of these Chinese had their bones exhumed and re-interred in the land of Sinim. As a child I once drove with Father and Mother to visit Mr. Henrici, the venerable then-head of the Economite Society. What I remember is that I was dressed in Highland costume, kilts, cairngorm and all, and lost my filibeg.

Only my father and the president, Dr. H. H. George, came from Northwood with the college to Beaver Falls. Since I was only nine months old at the time, and have no recollections of the Northwood home, I never thought of Ohio as my native state, or as the "pit of the rock" out of which I was digged. When the hegira from Northwood to Beaver Falls took place, Father and the two oldest sons, Ernest and Robertson, drove across Ohio in the family carriage. The family horse then was "General" Hunter, successor to "Colonel" Hunter, and named after the general who was in command of Union troops at the time of the battle of Monocacy, when Jubal Early made his great raid into Maryland in 1864. Father and my brothers had passed East Liverpool on their long drive, and were following the road by the Ohio River toward Beaver, when they saw bearing down on them in the distance a train. Hunter had never seen a locomotive, and all were apprehensive as to his reaction. Father took him out of the shafts and fastened him securely to a telegraph pole, and all stood back to see what would happen. Presently the locomotive came roaring along, sparks flying from the smoke-stack, and the ground shaking. Hunter never lifted his head! Fatigue had taken all the fear and fight out of him.

But Hunter was not always so meek. Father liked a good horse, and from all accounts Hunter was a magnificent animal, powerfully and gracefully built, jet black, with a white star on his forehead. On one of the early days at Beaver Falls, John Eccles, the colored student who lived in our attic and looked after the stable, was driving the family, with the exception of my father and my sister Wilhelmina, to the church on Main Street. Hunter took a fright at a fire engine and dashed down the street, overturning and smashing the carriage, and throwing everyone into the road. I was the baby, but wrapped securely in the arms of my nurse, "Alabama Mary," I suffered no injury. Father and my sister were just coming out of the church when they saw Hunter charging down the street, dragging the shafts at his heels. We were taken for first-aid into the brick house where the Brierleys lived. That was the beginning of a long and pleasant friendship between our families.

After the runaway, Mother refused to drive again behind the high-spirited and dangerous Hunter. Hunter was sold to a farmer, and Father purchased our new horse, Billy, a fine and very fast roan, a three-year-old. Mitchell, undertaker and blacksmith at New Galilee, commended Billy to Father as the most gentle of horses, but the first time Father took Mother out behind Billy he performed in a worse manner than Hunter had. Father drove him back to New Galilee and told Mitchell that Billy would never do, and that he must take him off his hands. Mitchell protested that there must be some mistake; that he had brought Billy up from a colt, and was sure there was nothing bad about him. He asked Father to give him another chance, saying that if, after the second trial, he was unsatisfactory, he would take him back.

The result was that for fourteen years Billy was our family horse, a friend to us all, and, although full of spirit, never once misbehaved in any way. Not many years ago, I happened to be preaching in the New Light Covenanter Church in Darlington. At the close of the service a woman came forward and identified herself as the daughter of the Mr. Mitchell of New Galilee who had sold Billy to Father. She went on to say how, when she was a child about three years of age, she was found missing one day at the house. After long search they found her asleep in Billy's stall, lying just in front of his hind hooves, but the wise animal for more than an hour had never moved lest he should trample the child.

The last chapter in Billy's career was a somewhat inglorious one. One by one, the four brothers in their turn, as the years went by, looked after Billy, and at this time it was my turn, being the youngest son. On a nice September morn, I went to the gate in the pasture to call Billy in to feed him and curry him. I called as the people were wont to do at that time when they called a horse, "Cope, Billy! Cope, Billy!" I can still see Billy as he came up through the mist of the September morn toward the gate, the white star showing on the black of his forehead, but I noticed at once that there was something odd about him. During the night the students from the college had got hold of Billy and shaved his tail, leaving just a tuft at the end. This, of course, ruined Billy's appearance, and made him look half lion, half jackass. At that time there was quite a business in wigs for horses, as well as for men and women. My brother Robertson went up to Pittsburgh to what was known as the Office of the City Fall Master, where they dealt in such things, to purchase a tail for Billy. When an attractive young woman came forward and asked him what he wanted, Robertson replied, "I want a tail."

In due season the wig arrived at Beaver Falls. It was a

grand sweeping tail, much more stately than Billy's own tail had ever been. Whenever we drove out, it fell to me to lace the wig onto the tail, and I remember how the flies would bite me as I ran the laces through the seemingly endless eyelets and lashed the false tail to the real tail. One day my oldest brother Ernest came down from Edgewood, where he was the minister of the church, to take Mother for a drive. Just before they entered the culvert under the railroad at Wallace's Run, they turned aside to let a funeral procession, returning from Grand View Cemetery, pass them. Just at that time Billy was "feeling his oats" in the crisp autumn air, and exalted his tail. In some way the false tail had become loose, and Billy's real tail, with the tuft on the end of it, waved in triumph over the ignoble false tail. As the chief mourners looked out of the windows of the funeral carriages, they were struck with amazement and then broke into laughter. Thus mourning was turned into mirth. We hired the county detective, Lazarus, to run down the perpetrators of this outrage, but never a trace of them was found. Perhaps some of those who had a hand in this work of darkness may chance to read this chapter, and if so, it is not too late yet to make a confession. *"While the lamp holds out to burn, The vilest sinner may return."*

With Mother, Wilhelmina, Albert, and Alabama Mary, I made my advent into Beaver Falls by train. Our house near the college not being finished, we took up our abode in what was called the "Shanty," the summer cottage of the Beaver Falls banker, John T. Reeves. Of that first home in Beaver Falls, I, of course, have no recollection, but the tradition is that they had great difficulty in restraining me from devouring the multi-colored caterpillars which swarmed in the land. One night a thief broke in and stole Father's watch and wallet, in which was money for paying the workmen on the new house. Father and Mother had the impression that they had been chloroformed. Be that as it was, the watch and the money were gone. Father's pantaloons were discovered in Dead Man's Hollow, across the Beaver River. Weeks after, a detective overheard a man in a New Castle saloon boasting how he had robbed a house at Beaver Falls. This led to his arrest and the recovery of the watch at a pawn shop. How that gold watch was impressed upon my childish mind! I can still see it in Father's hand as he would open it to see the time of day. On the back was a finely wrought Swiss chalet on the shore of a lake.

In the late autumn we moved from the "Shanty" into our new home, Fern Cliffe. It was a large, handsome, three-story frame house, with dormer and bay windows, capacious attic and cellar, a latticed back porch, and a conservatory with red, green, blue, and amber glass in the windows. The lumber for the house had been personally selected by Father. The house was pleasantly situated a hundred yards down from the college buildings and on the brow of the hill overlooking the river. Back of it was the neat barn for the horse and the cow, and the very large chicken house. Mother came from a beautiful home in Scotland, and was determined to make Fern Cliffe an attractive home. The house was well set, with southern exposure, looking up toward the college. Graceful, winding asphalt paths, the tar of which would get hot and soft in summer under our bare feet, led down to and around the house. I have abiding memories of the attic, where I used to lie on rainy days reading the "Youth's Companion" or, when still younger, standing on the rockers of the huge family cradle with my brother and pretending it was a ship at sea.

The huge cellar, too, was a favorite resort. In one part was the "inside" cellar, where were the bins for the apples. The apple I liked the best was what we called the Golden Russet, one I never see now. Often on a winter's night I would be sent down to fetch up the apples to eat around the fireplace in the living room before we went to bed. Just near the bottom of the cellar stairs there was a very dark place, and how my heart used to beat for fear lest a lurking robber should leap out upon me. In the coal cellar was the big furnace in which we used to heat the poker red-hot to burn holes for the bolts in our sleds so that we could make a bobsled of them. I can hear the sizzle as the poker burned its way through the back of the red sled, and even now I can smell the burning wood.

At the head of the cellar stairs, just inside of the door, hung a dreaded and most important item of equipment of our home. This was the "taws," which Mother had imported from Scotland. The taws consisted of a long yellow strap cut into tails at one end, and with a handle at the other. When guilty of some infraction of home rules, I would sometimes hear the command, "Clarence, bring the taws," and with dragging feet I would go to fetch the taws, and ere long would feel the bite of its tails on my outstretched palm. However, it was not often resorted to and for that reason was all the more respected. The year my mother died, my sister and her two children came to be with her at Beaver Falls. Albert Joseph, then seven, now a professor at Harvard, had misbehaved, and my sister sent him for the taws. Albert Joseph got the taws, but, instead of bringing them to his mother, brought them to his grandmother, who promptly hid them under the mattress. Thus Mother's last use of the taws was to hide them.

The new college building was an imposing and handsome structure. It had three stories, crowned by a cupola and a pinnacle. The chapel was on the second floor, the classrooms with their large windows on the first two stories, and the two literary societies, a never-missing part of a college building in those days, the Adelphic and the Aletheorian,

with their fine furnishings, at either end of the third story.
On the outside, between the two society rooms, was an open
gallery with iron balustrade. In the intermission the students would wander to and fro in that gallery, especially on a
moonlit night, and many a happy romance and many a happy
home had its beginning there. Although the college body
was small, the students came from all parts of the country.
Dick McCloskey came from under the very walls of Harvard
at Cambridge, and the Johnstons from far-off Seattle. There
were always a few colored students from the South. There
were three Hebrews, the Greenberg brothers, from Russia;
two Syrians from Beirut, and a swami from India. The for-
eigners whom I most clearly recall were two Chinese students, Huie Kin and Jim Linn. They lived in a house near
the entrance to our grounds, and when the "second bell"
was ringing in the college tower we would see them flying up
the path toward the college, their pigtails streaming out behind them. Jim Linn died early; but Huie Kin went through
Lane Theological Seminary at Cincinnati, and became in
time pastor of the Chinese Presbyterian Church in New
York. He married a New York woman of good Dutch Reformed family, and his sons later occupied high posts in the
Chinese government.

Our family left Beaver Falls for California before I was
ready for college, and I was thus the only one of the family
who was not a student at Geneva. Yet, in a sense, I was born
and brought up in the college. One of our early ambitions
was to walk in our bare feet clear around the college building by way of the stone ledge under the windows. As children we went eagerly to listen to the essays, orations, decla-
mations, and debates which were the solid menu of the literary societies of that day. Even now I can see William
H. Coverdale, who became president of the American Export
Lines, delivering his oration on Cortez; my brother Robert-

son commencing his speech on Napoleon, with the words: "It rains"; William H. Cox telling of the relief of Lucknow, and how the dying Highland girl, having heard before all others the skirl of the bagpipes, raised herself on her pillow and called out to those around her: "Dinna ye hear? The Campbells are coming!" Still I can hear another of those young orators—a splendid, black-haired youth from the country, who made a sad shipwreck of his life and promise, even in his college years—repeating the lines from "Locksley Hall," describing a state which then seemed not far off, but, alas, now so far distant:

> *"Till the war drum throbb'd no longer,*
> *And the battle flags were furl'd,*
> *In the Parliament of Man,*
> *The Federation of the world."*

Over the rostrum of the Aletheorian Society there was painted in great golden letters the Latin motto, *Ars Longa, Vita Brevis."* I was told it meant, "Art is long, but life is fleeting." My childish mind could not take that in then; but now, as the years slip by, I begin to catch the significance of that legend I used to read on Friday night over the platform of the Aletheorian Society. Yes, that is true. Art, in the sense of living well, is indeed long. The worthy deeds of the good life remain. "Their works do follow them." But the time for living the good life and sowing the good seed here on earth is brief. When sometimes I drive down to visit the college and the old home, and stand on the brow of the hill watching the Beaver flowing silently towards the Ohio, there come to me the words spoken of another river: "Stealing silently away, like the river of a man's life." Yes, Vita Brevis! At the entrance to the campus of one of our Southern colleges, there stands an equestrian statue of the founder of the college, a prince of industry, railroad builder, United States Senator, and a one-time candidate for the Vice Presidency on the Democratic ticket. On the base of the statue are cut these words:

"He worked as if he would live forever;
He lived as if he would die tomorrow."

CHAPTER V

BOYHOOD MEMORIES

OUR home at Beaver Falls was a wonderful place for the bringing up of children. We had two acres of land, an orchard between the house and the road, and woods on the hillside between the house and the river. Thus we had a spacious empire for our play. Our companions and playmates were, for
the most part, sons and daughters of the professors at the college. Just below our house, on the brow of the hill, was what
we called the grapevine tree. It was not a grapevine but a
venerable beech, closely entwined with vines. That was a
favorite resort, and each one of us claimed a particular
branch as his own. To climb high into that tree was one of
our earliest ambitions. An old photograph shows the heads
of the older children sticking out from the branches high up
on the tree while I, the youngest, stand disconsolately on the
ground.

As we grew a little older the Beaver River became our
place of adventure in winter and summer. Mother never
seemed to worry about our safety, although now and then
we took great chances. One of the winter thrills was what
we called "Hickory Bender." This meant skating over the
river when the ice was beginning to melt and heaved up and

down under us as we passed over it. We always had a boat, and Father taught us all how to manage it and how to swim. My one narrow escape from drowning came one day when we had been trying to entice Duke, our big St. Bernard and mastiff, to come down into the river where we were swimming. At length he ventured in, greatly excited, plunging up and down. Those near the shore got out of his way as quickly as possible, and the dog started for me, the farthest out. In a moment or two he was on me. At first I tried to get out of his way by swimming under water; but as soon as my head reappeared Duke was on top of me. Terrified himself, he was seeking safety by embracing me. His great paws with their claws scored into my back and I was beginning to go down, when Ernest saved me by getting astride Duke's back and in this position riding him into the shore.

One of the important appointments of our house was the big ten-gauge shotgun. I can see now the fine filigree of silver on it where the stock had been broken. Each of us felt himself a man when he was able to discharge that formidable piece of artillery. One memory associated with that gun is that of Father bringing down nine wild ducks on the river with one salvo from the two barrels; and another of seeing Father in the kitchen one night, by the light of the oil lamp, dressing and sewing up the deep wound on my brother Robertson's hand, made by the sharp teeth of a muskrat which he had shot by the river's bank, and then picked up by the tail, thinking it was dead.

Perhaps the biggest thrill of those early days at Beaver Falls were our encounters, sometimes altogether imaginary, with robbers and bandits. I can see myself sitting on Alabama Mary's knee in the stern of our boat, while Ernest and Robertson pulled for their lives at the two sets of oars, with the Long Tom shotgun ready for action. Behind us was a boat which had put out from the island that used to be in the river around the bend beyond Wallace's Run. The men were rowing hard and shouting at us—no doubt just a frolic on their part—but for us it was nothing less than the pursuit of pirates.

On several occasions our house, which stood far off by itself, was robbed. This always afforded the children great excitement. Coming home one day just at dusk from a picnic across the river, we found drawers out in bureaus, some of my mother's Scottish jewelry missing, and satchels slit open. The robbers evidently had been surprised by our return, for a box containing Mother's precious brooch had not been opened. As we were looking about, we suddenly heard Teza, our black Newfoundland, barking savagely as he rushed down the hillside. The thieves had apparently taken refuge in the cellar when we returned, and then made their getaway by a cellar window. On another occasion, when Father and Mother were in Scotland, we had seen two rough-looking fellows sitting under a tree in the adjoining college lot, sharpening what we took to be a glass-cutter. A few nights before, one of the cellar windows had been cut out. We were sure that on this night the robbers would return. After dark, Ernest, the oldest brother, assembled all of us in Mother and Father's bedroom. Our arsenal consisted of a coal bucket, ax, sledge hammer, a shotgun, and Teza, the dog. All lights were out, and Ernest, with the gun across his knees, sat watching at the open window. Albert and I, the youngest children, eagerly watched the proceedings from our little bedroom which led off from the other room, but no robbers appeared that night. Perhaps it was good for them that they did not.

Some unforgettable personalities crossed the stage of our life in those Beaver Falls days. One was Bill Dunn, who lived in a shanty up Steffin's Hill, and—when sufficiently sober—came in the springtime to dig in the garden. He always wore a derby hat, and had a stiff and bowed leg. Once, when he was taking his dinner in the kitchen and was asked to have another serving, he said to Mother, "I would go to heaven if I ate more beans!" Another was a tramp, James Quinn, who, on his regular rounds, stopped at our house every springtime, sleeping in the barn. He came of a good Baltimore family, and knew some Latin, for when he was cleaning one of the windows in the upstairs hall, he traced in the dust the words, *"In status quo"*—"in the usual condition." He ceased his annual visits when Father asked him to start painting the barn before breakfast. The last seen of James was in a chain gang on the Ohio roads.

Tramps were plentiful in those days, and they followed their regular beats. The greatest assortment I ever saw was when Coxey's Army passed through Beaver Falls during the depression of the 'Nineties. Coxey, a Massilon, Ohio, manufacturer, with a true regard for the poor and lowly, had a strange theory that the way to solve poverty was just to print and circulate abundant paper money. He collected an army that grew to perhaps five hundred men, and began the first "march on Washington." With some of the boys, I drove out to New Galilee to meet the oncoming host. It was a strange army indeed: many professional bums and tramps and, no doubt, many others out of work, who would have been glad to work if they had the chance, and who looked upon Coxey as their Moses. Coxey drove at the head of his column in an open two-horse phaeton, but the one who attracted the most attention was Coxey's Assistant Marshal, the "Great Unknown" Louis Smith, mounted on a magnificent bay charger. When the army reached Washington it assembled in front of the Capitol, where Coxey tried to read a proclamation from the Capitol steps, but was driven off by police. Grover Cleveland was then President of the United States.

Another local character not to be forgotten was the town cobbler, Valentine. His shop was in the upper part of Beaver

Falls, across from the rod and wire mill. He had formerly been a German sea captain, and was a man of native intelligence. Mother liked to converse with him in German. As the years went by, Valentine felt an urge for the sea again, and had a longing to visit the Fatherland. With that in mind, he began to build in the lot back of his cobbler's shop a small schooner. On Sabbath afternoons, on our way home from the Covenanter Church we boys used to stop at the shop and go around to the back to see what progress the schooner was making. Just as they probably jeered at Noah when he was building the ark, so we boys jeered at Valentine and his schooner. At length the craft was finished and hauled down to the Beaver below the Dam, whence it sailed into the Ohio, but when it reached the Mississippi the schooner was upset in a gale of wind. Poor Valentine had to go back to the cobbler's bench at Beaver Falls. When I think of him and his frustrated voyage across the ocean to Germany, there comes to my mind the record concerning King Jehoshaphat's voyage for the gold of Ophir: "Jehoshaphat made ships of Tarshish to go to Ophir for gold: but they went not; for the ships were broken at Ezion-geber." Yes, worthy old German cobbler, thy ship was not the only one which started for the Ophir gold of the heart's desire, and not the only one either that went not "for it was broken on the rocks."

Nor must I forget good old Captain Boyle, who lived in a farm house, just above the public watering trough. He had been a captain on the Ohio and Pennsylvania Canal, which ran from Rochester, Pennsylvania, to Youngstown, Ohio. The bed of this canal, and some of the locks, were still visible across the river from our home. It was on that canal that James A. Garfield rode the mules. Our teachers in school used to remind us of that, with the assurance that if we were obedient and industrious one of us, too, might one day become the President of the United States.

One rainy midnight in 1847 the packet boat *Evening Star* was leaving one of those long reaches of slack water which abound in the canal. When the horn sounded, Garfield, then sixteen years of age, roused himself out of his sleep and came on deck to take his turn at the bow. He picked up the end of a rope coiled on the deck and began to pull on it, but the rope had caught in some crevice. He gave it another pull, and then another, and still a stronger. Suddenly the rope gave way and he fell over backwards into the dark waters of the canal. He felt that he was going to drown, but instinctively he clung to the rope. To his great joy, he felt the rope grow taut in his hand, and quickly pulled himself up on the deck. After he had done his work in getting the boat through the locks, he picked up the rope and, going over to the side of the deck, flung it into the crevice in which it had caught. Once, twice, ten times, a hundred times, he threw it, but the rope did not catch again. The lad concluded that his life had been saved by the direct intervention of God. He felt that if God had in this way saved his life, there must be some other work for him to do than that of riding the mules on the tow path. He quit his job and went back to his home in the Ohio woods, where he found his mother on her knees before the fireplace praying for the welfare of her son. After he had greeted her he said, "Mother, I am going to make a man out of myself; I am going to get an education." He went through the academy which is now Hiram College, and then graduated at Williams College. Afterwards he taught at Hiram, studied for the law, became a successful lawyer, and, when the Civil War broke out, a brigadier general, serving on the staff of the Western army commanded by General Rosecrans. After a distinguished record in the army, he was elected to Congress from Ohio. On the day after Lincoln's assassination, April 15, 1865, an angry mob, ready to wreak vengeance on any persons who had criticized

61

Lincoln or the administration, had assembled on Wall Street in front of the Custom House. Suddenly a man in officer's uniform appeared on the balcony, waving a bit of paper in his hands. At once men in the mob down below began to call to one another, "Keep still! Another message from Washington!" But it was from a higher source than Washington. When the crowd was silent the man lifted his hand and, quoting the words of the Psalm, said: " 'Clouds and darkness are round about Him! Justice and judgment are the establishment of His throne!' God reigns, and the Government at Washington still lives!" The crowd was deeply moved by the words, and the threatened riot never occurred. The speaker was James A. Garfield, the lad who started on the path to success and the Presidency of the United States when his life was saved that night on the Pennsylvania Canal.

It was on that same canal that bluff old Captain Boyle had operated a packet boat. Captain Boyle, perhaps to remind the natives of his dignity as a former captain on the canal, always wore a white "biled" shirt. The Captain liked to talk to children. One day he told my brother Albert and me that if we put salt on a robin's tail, we could catch that harbinger of the springtime. The next morning, with our pockets filled with salt, we sallied forth into Boyle's lot, the meadow where we pastured Billy, and began our eager pursuit of the elusive robin. We showered abundant salt over the meadow, but about noon returned disappointed to the house, without salt or robins. The rest of the family smiled at us at the dinner table, yet we never held it against the old Captain, nor was our faith in human nature shaken.

CHAPTER VI

FIRST RELIGIOUS IMPRESSIONS

I received my earliest and most abiding religious impressions where they are always first received, in the home. Family worship was universal in the homes of our neighborhood, and we had "worship" every morning before breakfast and at night before going to bed. Father would say to one of the children, "Bring the books," whereupon the black-bound Bibles were brought from the shelf in the dumbwaiter which now serves as a closet. After we had sung a Psalm we then read around the circle the verses of the chapter for the day, after which we knelt for the prayer, by Father when he was at home, or, if he was away, by Mother. My first lessons in religion and in reading I had on those mornings at family worship, sitting on my father's knee as he, with his long forefinger, pointed out the words to me. The 121st Psalm was a favorite. We always sang that great "Traveler's Psalm" when any of the family was starting off to college, or on a journey. The benediction of that family altar has, I am sure, followed all of us through life thus far, and will, I hope, follow us up to the gate of heaven. Father was wont to conclude his petitions at the family altar with the prayer, "May we all get home at last!" Still on life's pilgrimage, the children who re-

main can hear the music of that grand 121st Psalm as we
sang it in the Scottish metrical version:

> *"I to the hills will lift mine eyes,*
> *From whence doth come mine aid*
> *My safety cometh from the Lord,*
> *Who heaven and earth hath made."*

The most treasured recollection of my mother's religious training is that of her singing by our bedside at night
in her clear, sweet voice the words of the hymn,

> *"There is a happy land,*
> *Far, far away."*

On Sabbath afternoons in the springtime and summer
mother took us down to a moss-covered rock under the sas-
safras trees on the hillside and told us the deathless tales of
the Bible. She had a little red-bound hymn book out of
which we sang with her some of the hymns. Covenanters
were not supposed to sing the hymns; only the Psalms of
David, and those Psalms are, indeed, the sweetest music this
side of heaven. Yet Mother was always free in her religious
life, and did not hesitate, on occasions, to sing the hymns. I
am sure that the singing of those hymns on the summer afternoons on that moss-covered rock on the hillside in the long
ago did much to introduce us to the warmth and tenderness
of personal religion.

We worshiped in the Covenanter Church in Beaver
Falls, two miles distant from our home. It was a dignified,
churchly building, with stone steps winding down from the
two entrances, a little grass plot in front, and enclosed from
the street with an iron fence. The pulpit alcove had a blue

dome, studded with stars. In those days the church was always filled, for the whole student body of the college, as well as the Covenanter families in the town, attended the services. There were no rented pews, but every family had its own pew. Ours was halfway down the aisle, on the right side of the center block. I can close my eyes now and see the different families in their pews. Just behind us sat the family of Dr. George, the president of the college. Over on the other side, Deacon White, with his long beard; the family of Professor Johnston, and the Downey family. Just alongside of us sat the McAnlis family and the Culbertsons. On the far aisle, against the wall, was the Paisley family. One of the boys had an armless sleeve, the consequence of "jumping" a freight train. They had a dark-haired daughter, too, a rarely beautiful young woman. Far in front sat a family with a half-witted daughter, who kept turning her head to gape at the congregation behind her. Nevertheless, she had wit enough to learn by heart the whole of the Larger Catechism. Most of us stopped with the Shorter.

The pastor of the church was an able and devoted man, Dr. R. J. George. At the time for the service to commence, he would come down our aisle clad in Prince Albert coat and white tie, his Bible held in his left hand and pressed against his breast; his head bent slightly to one side. The only two sermons the text of which I still recall were one on Acts 27: 44, from the story of Paul's shipwreck: "Some on boards and some on broken pieces of the ship. And so it came to pass that they escaped all safe to land"; the other a sermon for children from I Kings 17: 13, "Make me thereof a little cake first." That text naturally appealed to a boy. On an August day in 1933, on one of my journeys in the footsteps of St. Paul, I stood on the cliffs of St. Paul's Bay on the Island of Malta, looking down on the scene of Paul's shipwreck, so vividly described by Luke in the Acts, and thought of that sermon heard in my childhood in the Covenanter Church at Beaver Falls on that text, "And so they escaped all safe to land."

The great occasion in our church life was the semi-annual celebration of the Lord's Supper. For this commemoration a visiting minister always came to assist the pastor. The solemnities began with a fast day on the Friday before the Communion Sabbath. Then on Saturday afternoon came the Preparatory Service, after which we marched forward to receive the "Tokens" which admitted us to the Lord's Table on the Sabbath. The Tokens were not metal, as in the old Scottish days, but a card on which were printed the words of our Lord, "This do in remembrance of Me." Then on Sabbath morning came the great celebration. First the "Action" Sermon, designed to warm our hearts with repentance, faith, and love as we came to the Table. Then the "Fencing" of the Tables; that is, stating the qualifications for a worthy partaking of the Communion and giving warning to the impenitent and those living in sin or "secretly trusting in their own merits," lest so coming, they should "eat and drink damnation to themselves."

After this a Psalm was started, and about the time the second or third verse was reached, the families began to file out of their pews and take up the solemn march down the aisles to the Tables. The long Communion Table extended across the front of the church between the pulpit and the front pews. At one end of the Table there stood hunch-backed Elder Paisley, soberly clad in broadcloth, to whom we handed our Tokens. There were generally four Tables; that is, four sittings at the Communion Table. Our family, as a rule, joined the procession to the third Table. The Psalm most frequently sung by the congregation as they went swaying down the aisles was the 45th:

"Behold the daughter of the King
All glorious waits within;
And with embroideries of gold,
Her garments wrought have been.

She shall be brought before the King
In robes with needle wrought;
Her fellow-virgins following
Shall unto thee be brought."

I have officiated at the great Communion Service which opens the annual General Assembly of the Presbyterian Church. I have been stirred by the sacramental occasions in the three churches where I have served as minister. I have witnessed the gorgeous and pompous celebration of the mass in St. Sulpice in Paris, and the grand celebration in St. Isaac's Cathedral of the Orthodox Church, in what was then St. Petersburg; but never have I seen any Communion Service which so moved me as those commemorations in the Covenanter Church of my boyhood. The Covenanters had bled, suffered, and died to get free of the rites and liturgy of the English Church. Their communion celebration had no bell, no incense, no gown, and no organ; nothing of that nature; yet, in very truth, as I have just described it, it was poetic, symbolic and ritualistic in the highest degree. The particular communion phrase which still lingers sweetly in my memory, and one which I use whenever I administer the Communion myself, was that from the Song of Solomon, "Eat O friends; drink! yea, drink abundantly, O beloved." Yes, those stern old Covenanters had in them, unconsciously, all the poetry and mysticism of true religion.

When I was eleven years of age I united with the Church. I have heard men say, "I joined the church when I didn't know what it meant, or what I was doing." I could never understand that. The sublime mystery of the Trinity, the Atonement, the Life hereafter—that, of course, is too great and high, even for the mightiest intellect; and as for the majestic fact and truth celebrated at the Lord's Supper, the death of Christ for our sins, as for that, the very angels, Peter said, "Desire to look into it." Yet, in a certain sense, I certainly knew what I was doing when I united with the Church. I knew that I was trying to draw nigh to God; that I was giving my heart to the Saviour of men; and that I was associating myself with the followers of the Lamb of God in all ages, on earth and in heaven. I was not urged by my parents to join the Church, but was told how great and high a privilege and how great a duty it was, to confess the name of Christ before the world. In the little bedroom off the bathroom in our house, I knelt by the bedside and gave myself to the Lord. On the Communion Sabbath, having been examined by the pastor and the Session, and having answered satisfactorily the questions of the Shorter Catechism, I joined the procession down the aisle and sat down at the Communion Table. "I sat down under his shadow with great delight, and his fruit was sweet to my taste." And sweet ever since has it been.

CHAPTER VII

MY FIRST TEACHERS

FERN Cliffe, our home on College Hill, was beyond the bounds of the town of Beaver Falls, and for that reason we were sent first to the brick schoolhouse in Chippewa Township, about a mile and a half from our home. It stood well up the hill on the road to Darlington. When we set out for school in the morning, Mother gave us a verse for the day, such as, "See that ye fall not out by the way"; or, "My son, if sinners entice thee, consent thou not." We went down the road to the brick house, and then across a cornfield to the lane; down the lane, across a bridge, and up the hill to the school. It was the conventional "Little Red School House," of which so much was to be heard and sung in later years of "one hundred per cent Americanism." The big door had a huge lock and a latch on it; in the rear were the larger benches where the big boys sat, and where they cut deep niches in the lids of their desks with their jackknives. In the center was the iron stove, into which, from time to time, some mischievous boy would throw a piece of rubber to give us an unpleasant odor. Along the wall at the back were the hooks for coats and caps, and in front was the teacher's desk and platform, with bell on the desk. Dangerous looking rods were leaning against the wall in the corner for use on the backs of the bad boys.

There were little charts for the smaller children, displaying the cat in eager pursuit of the rat, and birds drinking out of the brook and lifting their heads heavenward. On the blackboard in front there was generally a verse from the Bible, most frequently one from the Book of Proverbs. Every Friday afternoon we had a "spelling bee." We were divided into two hostile camps and stood with our backs against the wall and tried to "spell down" the other side. Behind the schoolhouse was a coal shed, and to the left and right the privies, one for girls and one for boys. One of our favorite games was what we called "Andy Over." Two teams lined up on either side of the schoolhouse and the ball was thrown over the roof. If it dropped uncaught on the enemy's side, that was a point for the throwing side. That was my first contact with what is called today the "Honor System" in education, for the scoring depended upon the honest count of the opposite, and unseen, side.

Down the lane beyond the schoolhouse was the Edwards home, where were three girls, Mattie, May and Bird, and two boys, Bert and Glover. The girls were dark-haired, all pretty, and all very nice. Now and then we had a "party" at their house, the chief entertainment at which was "Post Office," when, as a fine or forfeit, we had a chance to kiss one of the girls. Many a bashful youth had his first, perhaps his last, kiss in that good old game of "Post Office." Beyond the Edwards home was the Montague farm. When we did not have a cow of our own at home, Montague brought us our daily portion of milk. He drove a chunky, cream-colored horse, and I can see him still as he sat in his covered wagon with its little stove-pipe smoking on a cold day and a pipe smoking in his mouth; and, when he drew up by our back porch, turning the brass faucet on his huge tank of milk.

Montague had a bull, and the people of the vicinity, when occasion demanded, drove their cows down the lane to the Montague barn, where Mrs. Montague, a huge woman, armed with a formidable club, loosed the bull and stood guard over him until he had performed his part.

My first teacher at this country school was a man named Speer, who lived not far off. He had a quick mind; indeed, as events turned out, too quick. I remember chiefly how he would take his stand at the back of the schoolroom, when no classes were reciting, and, whenever he spied a boy engaged in some mischief, would slip noiselessly down the aisle behind him, seize him by the ear and drag him up to the platform for exhibition and punishment. Once he dismissed the school and led us on the run down to the railroad to view the remains of a man who had been struck by a locomotive. One year all the children of parents so minded in Beaver County, were marshalled for a march and demonstration in Beaver Falls in favor of a Constitutional Amendment outlawing the sale of liquor in Pennsylvania. Our division formed rank on Sixth Avenue in front of the Central Hotel, which was one of the chief dispensaries of whiskey in town. We all had our little flags in our hands and sang patriotic songs. Speer, our teacher, was visibly excited and agitated as he ran up and down our lines, getting us ready for the march. After the parade, he went home, threatened his family with a butcher knife, and then hid in the loft of his barn, whence he was taken to Dixmont, the State Asylum for the Insane, halfway to Pittsburgh.

My next teacher was a woman, "Cal" Harbison. What the "Cal" stood for I never learned. Perhaps it was for a very beautiful name, Calvina. She lived at the Harbison farm just across from the school. One night sheep-killing dogs went amuck in the Harbison fields, and the next day the whole school trooped over to view the gruesome remains of the mangled sheep. "Cal" Harbison was a comely woman in the thirties. On the "last day of school" she gave us the annual treat, apples and doughnuts. This was a part of the school ritual that no teacher ever dared ignore. "Cal" had no little trouble with some of the bigger boys who sat on the back benches. One of these was Pete Riding, the son of a broom maker who lived farther up the hill toward Oakdale. One day she forcibly ejected Riding from the schoolroom, and compelled him to take his books with him. When he had gone out she turned the big key in the lock. About fifteen minutes later we heard a smash and a crash, as Riding kicked in one of the panels of the door, and then, one by one, hurled his slate and books through the hole halfway across the schoolroom. It was a supreme, eloquent, and unforgettable gesture of scorn and contempt for all book learning.

Two miles farther up the road on which the schoolhouse stood was the Schwartz farm. They lived in a substantial brick house, and across the road was another farm with a frame house of unusual and graceful proportions. The owners were Germans, or Swiss, and no doubt the house was fashioned after a lodge or chalet in the Fatherland! It was a great day for Albert and me when we were permitted to spend the night at the Schwartz farm. Olin, one of the sons, set a trap for us one night, and in the morning we went home with a rabbit. The other son, Watson, a student for the ministry, and already preaching in a nearby Methodist Church, we would sometimes hear on a Saturday afternoon as he paced up and down in the attic over our heads, pronouncing aloud the sentences of his sermon.

My third teacher was "Old Maid" Kennedy, who kept a private school in a house just across the road from the end of our driveway. It was there that I encountered an interesting forerunner of the present "lie-detector." Some misdeed had been committed by a scholar, and, in order to discover the guilty one, "Old Maid" Kennedy had us go one by one into a darkened room, where we were asked to thrust our hand into a basin covered with a cloth. In the basin—we afterwards learned when we emerged from the room and looked at our hands—was a quantity of blueing. "Old Maid's" theory was that the guilty boy, reproached by his conscience, would be afraid to put his hand deep into the basin—and thus the absence of the blueing stain on his hand would point him out as the culprit. But, alas, the blueing began to play out, and the last boy, Rutherford Glover, when he came along and put his hand into the basin, received very little stain, and was thus proclaimed the "guilty one." Perhaps he was; but the lack of blueing on his hand did not prove it. Yet, the theory of the "Old Maid" was good, and unconsciously she was predicting a later and more serious lie-detector.

My next teacher was an exceedingly pretty blue-eyed woman who taught us in a private school in what had formerly been a church, not far from a brewery. Whenever I smell the hops and mash in the vicinity of a brewery, I am carried back by that odor—and smell is said to be the swiftest agent of memory—to that little frame schoolhouse hard by the Anderton Brewery.

By this time a four-room schoolhouse had been built on College Hill, and not far from our home. We therefore left the private school and were enrolled in this new borough school. Our teacher was Benjamin Franklin; but in appearance he did not resemble the rotund Philadelphia philosopher and statesman, but Uncle Sam himself. He wore a long-tailed cut-away brown coat, and an Uncle Sam gray beard protruded from his chin. He was by that time a veteran teacher, and this school was his last round.

He was a man of high character and ability who carried two weapons: one a long pointer, which he sometimes used as a javelin, hurling it clear across the schoolroom at

an offending pupil, never worrying about the risk of putting
out the pupil's eye; the other a long, black strap, slit into
tails at the end. This weapon he stored in the pocket of his
coattails; and I can see him as he thrust his right hand into
the depths of his pocket and drew forth that dangerous
weapon. I never felt the strap, but I once did feel the pointer
as he passed along the front bench, where a dozen of us sat
against the wall, and laid it across our shins. The boys who
felt the strap swore that the tails of the strap were loaded
with lead. Good old Benjamin Franklin ended his days in
the toll house on the Beaver Falls-Brighton bridge.

Benjamin Franklin was followed by a stalwart young
man, Thompson, who lived on a farm four miles in the country, and walked back and forth every day. My most vivid recollection of him is the day he gave a sound thrashing to two
boys who certainly deserved what they got. The next day
the fathers of the two boys appeared at the school to protest
the "hiding" this teacher had given their sons. Nothing
stands out more clearly in my school days' recollections than
the sight of the teacher, Thompson, standing at the schoolroom door confronting the two fathers, his shoulders
squared, his head thrown back and his face flushed, as he told
the two men, who apparently had made some threat against
him, that he was running that school. He plainly intimated
that he was ready to give the fathers a sample of what he had
given their sons, if they desired it. It was a memorable and
splendid exhibition of physical and moral courage.

My next teacher was a woman, a Miss Given, a high-
minded, somewhat typical "School Marm" of that day. Once
when she was giving us a lesson in anatomy, and was using
one of the charts, some of the boys snickered at the exposure
of the human organs; whereupon Miss Given, her face
flushed with indignation, paused, and then slowly, and with
the greatest effect, rebuked the boys by repeating the words

of St. Paul to Titus, "Unto the pure, all things are pure."
Miss Given was followed by my last Pennsylvania teacher,
Mrs. Newton Long, widow of one of the professors at Geneva
College. I think she did more for me, in a way, than any of
my teachers. She tried to introduce us to good literature by
reading to us for a half hour each day from some worthy
book. Not only that, but she invited a few of the scholars to
come forward and read aloud to the others in the schoolroom. I was one of those boys, and it was an important day
for me when I was asked to read to the others.

The college atmosphere about us was a stirring and
stimulating one for youth. Father had a—in those days not
so common—"magic," or stereopticon, lantern, and on occasions gave an illustrated lecture. My brother Ernest generally operated the lantern in the gallery in the chapel of
the college. The gas was secured, and the light, from two
big tanks which stood alongside the lantern. On the afternoon of one of these lectures, the students had turned the
stop cock on the two tanks, and in the midst of the lecture
the light began to fail. Ernest called over the gallery to my
father on the platform, "Pa, the gas is giving out!" This incident, and Ernest's expression, were featured in the next
issue of the college paper. My brothers Ernest and Robertson tried their hands, too, at the lecture business; but the
most ambitious effort in that line was that of "The Three
Rising Stars." These "Three Stars" were Henry George, son
of the president of the college, my brother Albert, and myself. Our first entertainment was at Homewood, three miles
up the Beaver River, where we held forth in a schoolhouse.
Henry and Albert ran the lantern, another boy took the
"gate," and I delivered the lecture. The lecture consisted
of a series of views showing the incident at Mahon in the
Balearic Isles, when the Captain of the frigate *Constitution*
pointed a musket at his son, who had climbed to the top of

the mast, and commanded him to leap into the sea, because the boy had become dizzy and was sure to fall if he tried to come down the yards. "Jump, or I fire, he said." I quoted George Pope Morris's poem "The Main Truck, A Leap for Life," commencing

> *"Old Ironsides at anchor lay*
> *In the harbor of Mahon"*

We had some comic scenes, too—one of a man trying to ride a greased pig. It was an early version of the moving pictures. The motion was secured by moving the slide up and down in the lantern. Our next expedition was to New Galilee. We brought along part of our school drumcorps, and marched around the town before the lecture in good old-fashioned, patent-medicine style, trying to advertise our "show." When the time came for our performance, the schoolroom had in it a Negro hired man, a woman and child, and perhaps a few others; but that bothered us not at all, nor dimmed our ardor. This lecture experience, if somewhat presumptuous, was good training for the three boys and their future work in life.

Among my most pleasant memories of Beaver Falls is that of the annual trip to the farms at the nutting season. One farm we used to visit was the Burnison place on the south side of Beaver County, some miles out from what is now Monaca, but then Phillipsburg. To get there we had to cross the Ohio in a ferry. Those trips across the Ohio on our way to the farm gave us, I am sure, a bigger thrill than our first trip across the Atlantic Ocean. The Burnisons had two dogs, Shep, a fine collie, and Brave, a mongrel. These dogs ate, played, hunted, and slept together; but if one of them was caressed, the other at once bristled up and a fierce fight was in hand. The Burnisons had what I have not seen since, a dog churn. With dejected mien and tail close in, the dogs had to tread the inclined and moving platform which worked the churn. Churning day was on Thursday, and Shep and Brave got to know the calendar as well as the rest of the family, and when the day came round they would often disappear into the woods.

Another favorite place was the James McAnlis farm, four miles beyond New Galilee. We made our start early in the morning when the mists were lifting from the Beaver River. Billy was hitched to the spring wagon, and Teza, our Newfoundland dog, would leap up towards Billy's nose, while the horse flattened his ears and thrust down his head in a menacing gesture. Out to Wallace's Run we drove; then up the long hill to Summit Cut; downgrade to Galilee; and then out to the crossroads where the schoolhouse stood under the trees, and from there down the lane to the farm. On one of these trips Billy got loose in the barn one night and found a bagful of linseed oil, with very disastrous laxative effects. When we returned from these expeditions our spring wagon was well filled with sacks of walnuts, butternuts, hickory nuts and chestnuts.

Happy, happy memories!

CHAPTER VIII

CALIFORNIA

An important chapter in life opened for me when our family left Beaver Falls for California. My father, for some years then professor emeritus, was in poor health. After an examination his doctor had said to him, "Go to Redlands and live twenty years." He did live seventeen years, but only one of those years at Redlands. No Forty-niner could have started for California with more expectation or enthusiasm than we did on that September evening in 1894. When we had stopped over Sunday in Denver, Father was minded to remain there and try that climate; but the rest of us raised a rebellion. For California we had started, and to California we must go.

Our first view of California was in the neighborhood of Truckee, where we began to see the red soil and the big pine trees. Years afterwards, when the train on which I was travelling stopped at Truckee, I went forward and fell into conversation with the engineer. He turned out to be a man from Beaver County, Pennsylvania, and had lived on a farm back of New Brighton. He told me that some years before he had felt a strong urge to return to Beaver County and re-visit the farm where he had been brought up, and taste again a

78

particular kind of apple which grew on a particular tree in the orchard. At his vacation time he made the trip back to New Brighton. But the visit was a disappointment. This was the way he put it: "The old farm was there; the orchard was there; the trees were there; the apple was there; but the boy was not." Ah yes, "The boy was not." Returning many times to California since that first visit, I have realized the truth of what that engineer said. The red soil was there; the great trees were there; the brown mountains were there; the ocean was there; the orange groves, the pepper trees and the eucalyptus trees were there; but the boy of 1894, the boy of wonder and enthusiasm, was gone.

When the train stopped at Sacramento, we all got out to stretch our legs; also Duke, our big mastiff, who rode in the baggage car. When the time came to get on the train again, a new conductor refused to let us put Duke in the baggage car. As the train was just about to start, Father and Albert remained on the platform with Duke, while Mother, Wilhelmina, and I were left on the train without tickets or money. Because of this mishap, we missed seeing San Francisco; but the family managed to get together again at a station farther to the south.

At Los Angeles we sat under the palm trees in what is now Pershing Square, then Central Park, while Father went up to our Aunt Nora's home on Orange Street to see if she could take us all in. Aunt Nora was a devout Catholic, the widow of Father's brother William, who had been a lumberman in Wisconsin, and then a successful investor in real estate in Los Angeles. Aunt Nora gladly took us all in. While Father and Mother went to look for a suitable house in Redlands, Albert and I, with Duke and the shotgun, went down to visit a Scottish uncle at Santa Monica. Uncle Patrick Robertson had suffered heavy financial losses through investments about Santa Monica. He had the vision of the future, but was ahead of his time thirty or forty years. Some time before, Father, who was one of the directors of the newly established First National Bank at Beaver Falls, had brought Uncle Patrick on to serve as the cashier of the bank. He slept in a little room in the rear of the bank, and on occasions, I would go down and sleep with him, looking with awe on the big revolver he kept under his pillow. At the Merchants' Hotel where he boarded, I remember listening to a very profane parrot.

After a few days at Santa Monica, we went to Riverside, where, at the end of beautiful Arlington Avenue, we spent a day or two with our Scottish cousin, Edwin Robertson, whose father, our Uncle John, had purchased one of the first orange groves in California. From Riverside we made our way to our goal and destination, Redlands. We met Father on the street, and Duke gave him a tremendous welcome, irrigating in his excess of joy, one of the old-time fruit stands, much to the indignation of the fruit vendor. Redlands was then a town about ten years old, and became well known in the East as a health and tourist resort, largely through the Smiley brothers of Lake Mohonk fame, who had built beautiful homes on the hills overlooking Redlands. From the heights west of the town, one commands what is perhaps the most magnificent mountain view in California. In front lies the ever-green orange orchards; away to the right towers the snow-crowned summit of San Jacinto; a little to the left of San Jacinto rises San Gorgonio, familiarly known as "Gray Back"; across the San Bernardino Valley one can make out on the face of the mountain the arrow above Arrowhead Springs; and far off to the northwest rises "Old Baldy," or San Antonio.

We found a pleasant apartment in a house in an orange grove on Terracina Avenue. The next day Albert and I enrolled in the Redlands High School. The principal was a one-armed Professor H. F. Wegener, teacher of science. Miss Frances Lewis taught English, and the two Gleasons (the assistant principal and his sister Katherine), taught Latin and mathematics. They were all exceptional teachers and superior personalities. I still have in my library the rhetoric book used in Miss Lewis' English class, and on occasions still quote some of the excellent prose and poetry found therein. It was in Redlands High School, too, that I had my first introduction to Greek art. We used as a textbook Gayley's *Classic Myths*. Gayley was then a professor at the University of California. That is another reference book to which I frequently turn. The students were mostly children of middle-class Eastern families who had settled in Redlands. There were just a few boys from well-to-do families. We played baseball and football. I was not heavy enough for the Y.M.C.A. or the town team, but scrimmaged as a scrub. I remember how, when Redlands was playing another team, I wore my football pants under my regular clothes, hoping that somebody would get hurt, and that I might be called into the game! There, too, I played on the basketball team. Basketball had only recently been invented by Dr. James A. Naismith, the athletic director in Springfield College, Massachusetts. One of the games I played in was a night game against Riverside. That must have been one of the first night games of any description. When I was in the air after the ball, a player crashed into me, and took all the basketball and all the football out of me for some time.

The big sensation of that high school year at Redlands was when one of the boys, a fellow named Squires, was caught with a yellow-back novel in his desk. The whole school was assembled, as the principal hailed Squires before him and, holding up the offending book which, no doubt, was quite mild literature compared with the best-sellers of today, reprimanded Squires and warned the rest of us.

A boy whom I particularly remember—I wonder if he still survives—was one with the odd name of Quinine. He was as odd as his name, but an upright, able fellow. We sometimes studied together and hunted together. Out beyond Mentone at the Green Spot, lived a Bostonian family, the Lodges. Bessie Lodge, a pretty blue-eyed girl, was in my class. She rode a grey horse the six miles to school every morning. Once when Quinine and I were hunting jack rabbits in the "wash" of the Santa Ana Canyon, we found ourselves near to the Lodge home. Both of us wanted to see the pretty Bessie; but neither had the courage to go up to the house. We therefore contented ourselves with discharging our shotguns, hoping that Bessie would come running to see what the uproar was. But no Bessie appeared.

The second part of that winter at Redlands we lived in a pleasant little cottage facing the mountains, and just adjoining what is now the campus of the University of Redlands. Below us lived two demure damsels who were in my class at school. Every morning Albert and I walked along the sweetly murmuring Zanca and under the pepper trees and the eucalyptus trees on our way to school; and always, generally just a little ahead of us, walked the two damsels, yet we never said a word to them, nor they to us. Maytime came, and we heard rumors of a custom new to us, how a girl would tie a May basket, filled with flowers, to the door of the boy of her choice. It was then his duty, or rather opportunity, to run after the girl, who was never too far off, and kiss her. What a thrill it was on that May Day evening, when there was a slight noise at our door, and one of the family, opening the door, found a May basket hanging to the doorknob, and in the basket a card with my name on it! I was pushed out into the night in pursuit of the May girl. I ran down the road by the Zanca and soon saw her ahead of me; but the nearer I came, the more frightened I became. At length, panting, I drew up alongside of her; but I am now ashamed to relate that I left that fine opportunity pass unused. All that happened was that I made some remark about the fine evening, and then walked for a little distance by her side. The other members of the family have always said that I caught the wrong person, some grown woman, and kissed her, much to her amazement and indignation; but the true tale is the above.

Horseback riding, hunting jack rabbits, trips to Arrowhead Springs, and Mill Creek Canyon, basketball and football —and so passed that happy winter at Redlands. There were literary and oratorical feats, too. Albert won the prize in an essay contest on the Indian Question, writing under the pseudonym of "Sitting Bull." I sometimes entertained the high school, or social gatherings, with Ben Hur's "Chariot Race," or "Spartacus to the Gladiators"—"*Ye call me Chief, and ye do well to call him Chief!*" We attended the little Presbyterian Church and sang in the choir, led by a resounding trumpet. There was one number which we rendered at Easter as an anthem, that fine old hymn, "Up from the grave He arose!" We had never heard of Easter in our Covenanter days at Beaver Falls; and the whole celebration, in the beautiful California springtime, seemed to us a wonderful thing. There were also first-class lectures and concerts. A blind Negro, advertised as the celebrated "Blind Tom," performed at the piano, and, after listening to another musician play a difficult composition, sat down and repeated it, supposedly having never heard it before. At the end he stood up, and with a foolish smile of delight on his countenance, applauded vigorously with the audience. A speaker who greatly stirred me was the then-noted Joseph Cook, of the Monday Lectures at Boston. He had a grand peroration at the close of his lecture, in which he compared Christ with famous teachers, martyrs, patriots, and philosophers. After he had described and praised each one of them, he dismissed them with the words, "Thou art efficient, but thou art not sufficient." Then came Christ. After telling the work of the Redeemer, he concluded the lecture with the words, "Thou art efficient, and Thou and Thou alone, art sufficient." That lecture taught me one thing, what St. Paul calls "the exceeding greatness" of the Gospel. However bright and clever may be the words spoken of lesser persons and on lesser themes, it is only when we come to speak of the Everlasting Gospel and the Eternal Son of God that we strike the grand and major notes of human thought and human speech.

Our first summer in California we spent in tents at Long Beach, now the fourth city of California, but then a village of a few hundred people. We bathed in the surf, fished in the early morning, and raced our horse "Coaly" up and down the beach. One day, my brother Robertson and I drove along the sands to San Pedro, where we saw a forest of masts in the harbor: fishing smacks, lumber schooners from the north, and a few ships from across the seas. We secured a boat and rowed out to Dead Man's Island, which appears in Dana's *Two Years Before the Mast*, the great story of early California.

At Long Beach I came close to a terrible tragedy of love, jealousy, and murder. One afternoon there was the sound of pistol shots at a cottage just across from where our tents were. When we got over to the yard we saw four dead bodies stretched out on the grass, their faces covered with handkerchiefs. A husband, separated from his wife, had appeared at the cottage where she was staying, shot her, two others, and then turned the pistol on himself. Verily, "jealousy is cruel as the grave: the coals thereof are coals of fire, which hath a most vehement flame."

A handkerchief over their faces! Why? Once before I had seen that, when a handkerchief was drawn over the face

of a naked man who had been drowned in the Beaver River.
Just a piece of cloth! But that piece of cloth over the face of
the drowned man, and over the faces of the murdered and
the murderer there on the grass under the pine tree at Long
Beach, was a tribute to the mysterious sacredness of life. Yes;
let the face of the dead be shielded from the gaping crowd.
O man! with all thy infamies, thou art not altogether a beast
as long as thou dost lay a handkerchief over the face of the
dead.

In order that my sister, Wilhelmina, who had finished
her junior year at Geneva College, might have an opportunity
to complete her college course, we removed from Redlands
to Claremont, where was the recently established Pomona
College. Our first introduction to the college had been the
previous winter when Father, Albert, and I drove from Redlands to Los Angeles for the Christmas vacation. In the
"wash" east of Claremont, we met a gentleman wearing gold
glasses, mutton-chop whiskers, with a keen scholarly air
about him, sitting in a little buckboard behind a spavined,
miserable-looking sorrel horse. It was none other than the
Professor of Latin at Pomona, Professor Daniel H. Colcord,
whom we came to know well the next winter.

Albert and I and the dog drove from Long Beach to
Claremont behind our splendid black horse "Coaly." Passing
through the town of Compton, I think it was, we saw on a
wagon the carcass of a huge mountain lion which had been
shot in the mountains nearby. When we reached Claremont
that night, and found Father at our new home, El Elesal, our
enthusiasm knew no bounds. Here, we said to one another,
would be our home until all of us had finished college. El
Elesal, which means "The Place of Peace," was a charming,
rambling, one-story house, set down by live oak trees and
under gigantic eucalyptus trees, in the midst of a ten-acre
orange grove. The owner was a Scotsman, a Mr. Palmer, who

had embellished the place with flower beds, palm trees, rock gardens, and a pretty little lodge or summer house. There was a windmill that pumped water into the reservoir for irrigating purposes. Albert and I looked after the grounds and irrigated the orange trees after our work at the college. It was there that I learned for the first time the faithfulness of nature and the regularity of the winds. Every morning about 10 o'clock, the sea breeze would come in and the windmill would begin to turn, and every afternoon about 3 o'clock, the mountain breeze would spring up, and once again the wheel would begin to turn.

Pomona College was staffed by Congregational ministers. Dr. Cyrus G. Baldwin was the president; Dr. Charles B. Sumner, the chief founder and supporter; Colcord, the Latin Professor; and Dr. Edwin Clarence Norton, the Greek Professor. Frank Parkhurst Brackett and George Gale Hitchcock, both laymen, were the very able teachers of astronomy and physics. The first winter I was there, Dr. Norton was absent, and his classes were taught by David Prescott Barrows, a graduate of the college in the first class and just back from a year of graduate studies at Columbia University. He was a young man of great enthusiasm, and afterwards became president of the University of California and a major general in the Army in World War I.

The most eccentric, and perhaps the most memorable of my Pomona teachers, was a Professor Clarence Eugene Blake, author of Greek and Latin textbooks, and who came out, as I remember, from the University of Vermont, to take some of Dr. Norton's Greek classes during his absence. He wore a little robin's tail cut-away coat, a stiff stand-up collar, and a black string tie. When he got up on his platform in the classroom in the morning, he would invariably lift up one foot, and then the other, and tap the soles of his shoes with a pencil to see if they were damp. He lived at Sumner

Hall, the girls' dormitory. Two of the students who earned their meals by working in the kitchen one evening got into a friendly dispute, and one pursued the other as he fled around the building. When they had circled Sumner Hall and had reached the kitchen door, near which was the wood shed, the pursuer saw one whom he took to be his adversary bending over the wood box, gathering an armful of wood. As he came up with him, he gave him a tremendous blow with an upraised plank on the most prominently exposed portion of his anatomy, and knocked him headlong into the wood box. Alas! It was not his adversary, but Blake, the professor of Greek.

Blake presided over a number of us, at what was supposed to be a "study hour." Sometimes he would go out and remain for quite a time, during which the boys raised an uproar. When at length he did return, he had a way of slowly and slyly pushing the door open, and then, bent over well, backing several feet into the classroom, when he would quickly straighten himself up and wheel around, and, raising a warning forefinger, would exclaim, "Now boys, no talking; no talking, boys!"

One day Professor Blake went out, and after a little I followed him. I wandered about for a few minutes in the hall, and then came back. When my hand was on the door-knob an unfortunate inspiration came to me to imitate the old fellow in his way of entering the classroom. Slowly, very slowly, I pushed the door open, bent over like a jackknife, and backed slowly across the room, almost up to the desk. Then I wheeled about and, raising my hand aloft, and imitating as best I could Blake's high-pitched voice, shouted, "No talking, boys! No talking!" But as I did so, I saw a look of consternation, and also suppressed glee, on the faces of my classmates. Alas! Blake had returned before me, and now, with amazement and fallen jaw, was watching my performance. It was one of those times when something had to be said. Just in front sat Jimmie Patten, who always wore sneakers. Pointing to him, I said to Blake, "May I see Jimmie Patten?" Blake, with a half-stupefied look on his face, nodded his assent; whereupon Jimmie and I went out, and soon were rolling over one another in the hallway. When we had composed ourselves somewhat, we returned with sober countenance to the classroom. At the dismissal bell, Professor Blake said to me, "Macartney, you will remain; I want a word with you." I thought this meant my Pomona College days were over. But this is what happened. Looking earnestly and admiringly at me, Blake said, "Macartney, the boys have been misbehaving when I went out, and you were trying to preserve order. That's it, isn't it?" Stupid, learned, innocent old Blake! I don't think my conscience permitted me to say that I was trying to maintain order in the classroom. All I did was to bow my head and retire in great joy.

There was high enthusiasm for athletics at Pomona College. I made a try for the track team, running the hundred-yard dash and the two-twenty. I was not old enough or strong enough to make the team, being then only sixteen years old, and still in the Preparatory School; but in one race I was fast enough to give Lucius Tolman and Frank Nance, our champion sprinter, and afterwards for many years, coroner of Los Angeles county, a run for their money. On the Fourth of July the next summer, and on the public road at Pomona, I ran as anchor man on a relay team made up of Pomona College boys, and we defeated in a quarter-mile race the pick of that part of Southern California. The other three on our team were Lucius Tolman, who became a chemist with the packing house, Wilson & Company; his brother Ruel, later the director of the National Collection of Fine Arts of the Smithsonian Institute at Washington, and Dick Lamb. I still have the photograph of that team.

If I had been a little faster, and a little less bashful and reticent, I might have been a champion sprinter. Thereby hangs a tale. I wanted to have a pair of blue running trunks cut out, so that Mother could sew them together for me. I drove "Coaly" down to Pomona three miles distant, and, somewhat embarrassed, asked a rather pretty sales girl in the chief store of that nature in the town, if they "cut trunks here?" She thought I was asking if they cut down prices on travelling trunks. She smiled and said she thought they might do so, and then conducted me to the back of the store and showed me an assortment of trunks! For some reason I was too overcome with modesty and bashfulness to explain that what I wanted was not a trunk for travelling abroad, but trunks for my thighs and hips, so that I could travel over the cinder path. When I rejected all the trunks she showed me, she called the manager, who took me up on the mezzanine floor and began to haul out divers trunks: box trunks, steamer trunks, all that he had in store. By this time I was in a cold sweat. It was only by the grace of God that I got out of that store without having put myself down for the purchase of a travelling trunk.

I was the captain of our class baseball team, but as the day drew nigh for the big game with one of the upper classes, I developed a boil, or carbuncle, on the back of my neck. I went down to old Doctor Hunt and asked him to lance it, so I could play in the game the next day. He quite properly said it was not ready for lancing, and dismissed me. In our class was a fellow, Samuel Howard Bowman, who had served time as an orderly in a San Francisco Hospital, and therefore considered himself an expert with the knife. With several other boys, I went down to the cabin where he lived and submitted to a painful cutting with his razor. I played in the game the next day, but was afflicted afterwards with a dangerously sore neck. I still have on the back of my neck the scar of that folly.

Speaking and debating interests also ran high at the college. The Seniors delivered orations at Chapel, and there was an annual exciting oratorical contest. The orators were trained by Dr. Colcord, professor of Latin. I can see him with his mutton-chop whiskers and gold glasses as he gave his annual address to the students on oratory. In illustrating inept gestures, there was a place where he described a man saying in the course of his speech, "Up to heaven, or down to hell," but in both instances pointing in the wrong direction. Once I saw him in the old shed, which then served as a field house for the athletes, putting Robert C. Owens through his oration. I can hear Robert say in the course of his speech, clenching his fists as he did so, how something was "changed from ductile clay to solid rock." Robert served for many years as law librarian in San Francisco. Other Pomona students whom I remember were Josiah Sibley, who lived in the tower of the college and rang the bell for the classroom hours; Fred Goodrich Athearn, a big fellow who played on the football team, ran the college barber shop, and also taught penmanship; the Fairchild brothers—one of them afterwards a well-known physician; Harrison G. Sloane, the pole vaulter; and others whom I cannot now name.

Through the school year we had concerts, lectures, and addresses by visiting speakers, ministers, and evangelists. The star concert was by one Herr Schott, a German baritone. It was to that concert that I first took a young lady. She was a classmate named Avis Smith, who afterwards married another classmate, Llewellyn Bixby of Long Beach. Herr Schott was a mighty singer before the Lord. His chief song was "The Two Grenadiers." Another that evoked great applause was one with the words in it, " 'Till the stars grow dim, and the leaves of the judgment book unfold." Avis and

I sat just near the door that opened onto a little veranda. There Herr Schott had a tub filled with ice in which floated beer bottles. I can see now the gleam of his vast shirt front as he threw back his great grey head and poured the beer down his throat. The beer was a great shock and scandal in college circles, for at Pomona in that day, none of the students drank, smoked, or played cards. Years afterwards, Dr. Brackett, then professor of Mathematics, told me that the beer was secured from the cellar of Professor Pearson, who taught music and Indian lore. Herr Schott produced an even greater shock when he gave a concert in the Congregational Church at Pomona, and had the same tub filled with ice and beer in the vestibule, where he regaled himself between his songs.

One lecturer came along who greatly stirred me with lectures on historical characters such as Frederick the Great and Mary, Queen of Scots. I have done a great deal of biographical preaching and writing in my day, and that Pomona lecturer did much to kindle that flame of interest within me. In the field of religion we heard the noted evangelistic singer, George C. Stebbins, the composer of "Saved by grace," "Saviour, breathe an evening blessing," and other well-known hymns. He was at his prime then as a magnificent baritone. Stebbins lived until 1945, when he was 99 years of age. Before his death I had some correspondence with him, and he remembered well that visit to the chapel of Pomona College. In the Congregational Church in the town of Pomona I had the good fortune to hear Ira D. Sankey, of Moody and Sankey fame. He was then far advanced in years; but as he sat at his little reed organ on the platform and sang, "There were ninety and nine," his voice rang out like a trumpet. It was in that church, too, that I once heard B. Fay Mills, then a great soul-winner and a most persuasive preacher. Mills fell from grace, lost his message, drifted into the morass of Unitarianism, found even that church not liberal enough for him, and set up some sort of a "Humanitarian" church at Los Angeles. He afterwards recanted his modernism and apostasy, and, in a moving scene, was re-established as a minister of the gospel by the Presbytery of Chicago. Like Dr. Lawrence Maclay Colfelt, the eloquent Philadelphia preacher, and not a few others "in the far country," he "came to himself," and "arose and came unto his Father."

A chapel speaker who made a deep impression on me was Charles Nelson Crittenton, the wealthy drug merchant of Chicago, who was brought to himself and to God by the death of his beautiful daughter. He founded in her memory the Florence Crittenton Home for young women who had gone astray. The second winter I was at Pomona College, one of my classmates, Hugh Vernon Eads, died. His funeral, at which I was one of the pallbearers, was to all of us a very solemn event. He was a grandson of James Buchanan Eads, who built the Eads bridge over the Mississippi River at St. Louis.

J. C. Furnas, whose book, *Voyage to Windward,* is an excellent biography of Robert Louis Stevenson, relates how when he was living at Samoa, Stevenson "joined the ravishingly beautiful Ide sisters" to teach classes in an Apia Sunday School for natives and half-caste children. One of these "ravishingly beautiful Ide sisters" came to Pomona College in my senior year in the preparatory school. She was tall, fair, graceful and indeed beautiful, and lived with Professor Norton's family. Another sister married the noted Democratic orator, William Bourke Cockran, whom I heard speak when I was a student at the University of Wisconsin.

In Dr. Norton's study there was framed on the wall a rather strange relic, fragments of a pair of cuffs and broken cuff links. When he was a young man driving a wagon one day near his New England home, a bolt of lightning struck the wagon, killed the horses, and severely shocked Norton. Most of his clothing was stripped from him. About all that was left was fragments of his cuffs and cuff links. His narrow escape from death convinced him that God had something useful for him to do in life. That is how he came to frame the links and the pieces of his cuffs, and hang them on the wall of his study as a constant inspiration to high living.

At the entrance to the campus of Pomona College is a memorial gateway. On the outside, greeting the freshmen as they enter college, are cut these words: "Let only the eager, thoughtful and reverent enter here." On the inside, as a farewell message to the seniors as they go out into the world, are cut these words: "They only are loyal to this college who, departing, bear their added riches in trust for mankind." Not many colleges would have much of an enrollment if they admitted only the "eager, thoughtful and reverent." But Pomona College in those days had a good proportion of eager, thoughtful and reverent students, and not a few of them have endeavored through the years to "bear their added riches in trust for mankind."

CHAPTER IX

DENVER

FATHER's health had not improved much during the two years' stay in California, and he resolved to try the air of Colorado. We spent the first summer that we were in Claremont in the mountains at what is now "Camp Baldy," where we had a happy and beautiful summer, living in tents on the banks of the brawling mountain stream, and exploring the canyons and mountains in the neighborhood. On one of our trips we scaled Old Baldy, where we saw the sun rise in magnificence over the Mojave Desert, coming out of his chamber like a bridegroom, and rejoicing like a strong man to run his race. At the end of the summer my two older brothers, Ernest, minister of the church at Edgewood, Pennsylvania, near Pittsburgh, and Robertson, who had just finished his course at the San Francisco Theological Seminary at San Anselmo, set out for graduate studies at Edinburgh, Scotland. Father and Mother, my brother Albert, and my sister then went on to Denver, where the brother and the sister entered Denver University. I demurred at being removed from Pomona College, and was permitted to stay behind for another year and finish my course in the Preparatory Department. I have always been glad that I stood out for that privilege. Our commencement night when we graduated from the preparatory school was to all of us a great event. I delivered an oration on Louis Kossuth, the great Hungarian orator and patriot. For this occasion I borrowed Bob Owens' long black cut-away coat.

At the end of the summer, having worked about Sumner Hall and in the apricot orchards, I followed the family to Denver. On the train was a young woman who had been visiting friends in Pomona during the winter, and who had been in our circle at the college. Norma Keenan was her name, and she came from Huntingdon, West Virginia. I wonder if she is still alive, and if she remembers that journey eastward on the Santa Fe. That fall I entered the freshman class at the University of Denver. Denver University was a Methodist institution, located at University Park, five miles out from the city. The professional schools, law, dentistry, and medicine, were in the city. The three buildings at University Park were University Hall (Old Main), where all the classes were held, the red stone Iliff School of Theology, and the Chamberlin Observatory, with one of the largest telescopes in America. There were few students in the academic department, and most of them came out every day by streetcar from Denver. The student body, on the whole, was not the equal in character, earnestness, and conduct of that at Pomona College. I suppose it was contact with city life that made the difference.

Two men made a lasting impression on us. One was the Chancellor, Dr. William F. McDowell—afterwards a bishop of the Methodist Church. He was then in the late thirties, and cast a spell of charm and inspiration over us. He lectured now and then on the French Revolution; but most of his energies were devoted to finances and to saving the University from being sold by the sheriff. In his speaking and preaching he had, to a marked degree, what used to be spoken of as "unction." In his chapel addresses he would rise on his toes and shake his fine head as he reached his climaxes. The other professor whose personality stands out through the mists of memory was Dr. Ammi Bradford Hyde, the professor of Greek. He was an extraordinary man, most eccentric in appearance and in speech. He wore a dark grey Prince Albert coat, displayed a fringe of grey whiskers about his chin, and carried his glasses on the end of his nose. His comments and "asides" made his classes an entertainment and an education in life, rather than in Greek. Most memorable and moving were his chapel prayers. He would throw out his long arms in front of him, the cuffs of his shirt far below the sleeve of his coat, and the palms of his hands turned heavenward, as if to receive the gifts of God, as he pled for us at the Mercy Seat.

On Sabbath mornings, my brother, sister, and I walked down to the Covenanter Church on Pearl Street in Denver, where the minister was Dr. Thomas Houston Acheson, a former student of Father's at Geneva College. He was no "Son of Thunder," but always brought "well-beaten oil" into the sanctuary, and was an illustration of the truth that even in one of limited parts careful study and meditation can produce a very worth-while sermon. In the evenings we went down to the Central Presbyterian Church, where tall and stately Dr. James E. Sentz preached what seemed to us able sermons to a vast expanse of empty pews. It was a singular church in this respect, that around the walls of the sanctuary were boxes, just like theatre boxes, enclosed with a brass railing and red velvet curtains, where, apart from the common throng, sat the nabobs of Capitol Hill. On our way to church one May evening, my brother and I saw posted in the window of the Rocky Mountain News a bulletin stating that Commodore Dewey had fought and sunk the Spanish fleet in Manila Bay. When we reached the church we passed this word on to Dr. Sentz. After the opening doxology, he said to the congregation, "I have just been informed that the Spanish fleet is at the bottom of Manila Bay. Let us stand and sing 'The Star-Spangled Banner'!' "

It was at Denver that I had the good fortune to see and hear one of the commanding personalities of that day, General William Booth, of the Salvation Army. I was too young fully to appreciate it then, but now I know that I saw and heard one of the most apostolic and influential personalities in the history of the Christian Church. As he stood there on the platform, clad in his long blue coat and crimson waistcoat, with his grey locks and splendid Roman nose, he looked like one of the Hebrew prophets.

At the end of the school year we gave up our house at University Park, and our parents and sister made a trip to the East. Albert and I were left behind to shift for ourselves, as Father believed in men working and supporting themselves. Albert secured a job at Leadville, the fabulous mining town, while I got a job on a ranch not far from Morrison, about fifteen miles out from Denver. It was chiefly an alfalfa ranch, but had also some cattle and horses. The ranch was owned and run by a man who had formerly been a ticket agent on the "Katy" or Missouri, Kansas and Texas railroad. He was a devout man and had prayer with the family and ranch hands every morning after breakfast. I was the only one of the hands, however, who knelt down with the family at the prayer. When I arrived at the ranch I was assigned a cot in the bunk house; but after a few days the rancher said to me, "You seem different from the rest of these fellows; I think you had better sleep in the house." I accepted his invitation, but soon regretted it, for I had a very small room and was tormented by mosquitoes. For this reason I soon moved back to the bunk house where I learned, but did not use what was called the "Bunk House Prayer":

"Now I lay me down to sleep;
Ten thousand bedbugs o'er me creep.
If one should bite before I wake,
I pray the Lord, his neck to break."

In the bunk house I was confronted at once with a moral struggle. Did I have the courage to kneel down in the room in the presence of those rough and profane men and say my prayers? It was hard at first; but I won the battle. Never did any of those men mock at me or interrupt me. There were some interesting and attractive characters among them, and with a different early environment and guidance, they might have filled important posts in life. But, alas! their only idea of a good time was to go to Morrison and get drunk, with the usual beastly accompaniments of drunkenness. One night, returning late from Morrison and well heated with whiskey, thinking I was sound asleep, they had quite a debate among themselves as to whether they should "wake Mac up and make him drink from the bottle." The one who put a stop to it and saved me from that ordeal was the roughest and most profane of the whole group.

Having told the boss when I came to the ranch that I could drive a team, although I had never driven anything but our family horse, I was assigned to drive a wagon in the alfalfa field. This meant not only driving the team, but also taking the hay as it was pitched up at me from either side of the wagon and loading it evenly in two sections, so that it could be carried up to the stack by the hay knives. I succeeded in getting the first load on; but when we were crossing an irrigation ditch the wagon upset, and I was demoted to the ground, where, a boy of eighteen, I was put over against a seasoned and hardened Irish rancher and had to hold up my side in pitching the heavy cocks of hay onto the wagon. There were plenty of rattlesnakes in the fields to break the monotony of that labor; but perhaps our most exciting experiences came on stormy nights, when the thunderstorms came rolling and rumbling down from the mountains, and we were routed out of the bunk house to cover the huge stacks with tarpaulins. It was like going aloft in a storm on a sailing ship, for the weighting logs had to be fastened to the brass eyelets in the tarpaulins, and to do this we had to go far down the sides of the towering stacks.

When I first came to the ranch I was asked the usual question, "Can you milk a cow?" The cowboys, who all knew how, but never admitted that they did, were exempted from this labor, which they considered unworthy of a cowboy. Unfortunately, I had milked the family cow at Beaver Falls, and, having been trained to tell the truth, I told the boss, when he asked me, that I could milk. I was therefore assigned to help in the morning milking, a task which began about five in the morning. For the first few days, when I awoke, my hands were so stiff and sore from holding the pitchfork, that I had to take each finger and unbend it.

The thing that bothered me most in my milking chore was the presence of the white-and-black bull in the corral. I would stone him away when I first began to milk, but was always careful to look from time to time around the cow's tail to see if he was in my vicinity. One week the bull disappeared for several days. At length he was located down in the bushes in a gulch, evidently suffering from some kind of distemper. He was driven back to the corral; and that night, after all the chores had been done, we proceeded to give Taurus a dose of castor oil. It was now getting dark, and I was the "lantern holder." The bull had been thrown on his side, one man having a rope on his hind leg and another on his horns, while the boss attempted to administer the castor oil. In the midst of this operation, the bull in some way managed to get to his feet, and seeing the light of the lantern, started for me. The ground sloped sharply towards the big corral fence. I traversed the distance between me and the fence in quick time, and in a moment was over the fence, gum boots, lantern and all, leaving the three men struggling with the bull in the darkness, and with profane words calling for the lantern and denouncing me for having deserted them. As for getting over that high corral fence, it was one of those times when you had to climb, whether it was possible or not.

On the Sabbath afternoons on the ranch I used to go high up on the mountainside, where I exercised my voice and cultivated the spiritual life, and, half-consciously, prepared for the work in life ahead of me, by reading passages from Isaiah and St. Paul. I recall particularly reading, as my voice rang out over the mountainside, the sublime fifteenth chapter of First Corinthians, the great passage on the immortality of the soul. "O death, where is thy sting? O grave, where is thy victory? The sting of death is sin, and the strength of sin is the law; but thanks be to God, who giveth us the victory through our Lord Jesus Christ."

At the end of that summer on the ranch I was thin, but hard as nails. On my last day I drove with the boss into Denver, where we delivered a load of baled alfalfa to the barn of a Denver merchant. In the alfalfa harvest there are three, and sometimes four, cuttings. The best cutting is the second. The boss was on the wagon, pitching the bales up to me where I stood in the door of the haymow, when the merchant appeared on the scene. He pulled out some of the hay from one of the bales and said to the boss, "That doesn't look to me like second cutting." That was what he had ordered. There was silence for a moment, and then, with a look of injured innocence, the rancher replied, "That's what you ordered, isn't it?" As if to say that it was unthinkable that he should give the merchant anything else but the second cutting which he had ordered. In reality, it was the third or fourth cutting. With the hay hooks in my hands I stood in the door of the haymow watching that drama of conscience. It had been a hard season for the boss on the ranch, and he had yielded to the temptation to gain a few dollars by delivering third or fourth cutting instead of second. That night the rancher paid me off on one of the streets in Denver. Forty dollars in gold, for my summer's toil. As he handed me the money he said to me, "Mac, I didn't tell that man, did I, that the hay was second cutting?" No, he had not actually told him that; and yet, in effect, when he answered with that question, "That's what you ordered, isn't it?" he had really said that the hay was second cutting. So I left him in the gathering gloom of that early September day, pondering deeply on the power of temptation and the reproach of conscience. The incident gave me a good illustration, which I have sometimes used when preaching on conscience, its exceeding high reward, and its inexorable reproach.

CHAPTER X

THE UNIVERSITY OF WISCONSIN

AFTER I was paid off by the rancher that night in Denver, with forty dollars in gold in my pocket, I joined my brother Albert, who had come down from Leadville, and together, armed with "scalpers' tickets" we set out for Madison and the University of Wisconsin. My brother Robertson, recently returned from his studies abroad, was now the minister of the church at Oconto, on Green Bay, and Ernest for several months had supplied the pulpit of Christ Church in Madison. They both thought the University of Wisconsin would be a splendid school for their younger brothers.

At Chicago Albert and I outfitted ourselves at the Hub store and boarded the *City of Virginia* for Milwaukee. Thirty-seven years later, I was crossing from the port of Los Angeles to Catalina Island. The steamer turned out to be the same *City of Virginia* on which we had made the night journey to Milwaukee so many years before. It had been brought through the lakes, down the St. Lawrence, through the Panama Canal, and up the coast to Los Angeles. Coming into Madison on the Milwaukee and St. Paul Railroad, and skirting Lake Monona, we had our first view of the dome of the Capitol as it rose over that beautiful city. We found a

pleasant home on Wilson Street, just a few yards from Lake
Monona. Longfellow never saw Madison, but he fitly described the town and the four lakes which surround it in
these lines from *The Four Lakes of Madison:*

> *Fair lakes, serene and full of light,*
> *Fair town, arrayed in robes of white,*
> *How visionary ye appear!*
> *All like a floating landscape seems*
> *In cloud-land or the land of dreams,*
> *Bathed in a golden atmosphere!*

Never can I forget the stir and interest of those first
weeks at Madison. The leaves were turning yellow and crimson; the autumn air was crisp, and the students came and
went in long procession up and down "The Hill," at the top
of which was "Old Main," a handsome building, nobly set,
looking over Lake Mendota and Lake Monona and down toward the State Capitol. On the lower campus, next to what
is now the beautiful State Historical Library, the football
team, which had achieved national fame under the coaching
of Phil King, famous Hebrew Princeton quarterback, was
practicing. The great football hero of those days at Wisconsin was the fullback, Pat O'Dea. He and his brother had
come from Australia, and that is how Pat was known as the
"Kangaroo Kicker." In a game with Northwestern University he made a drop-kick of sixty-two yards, the longest kick
on record. For many years after he left the University,
O'Dea was lost sight of; no one knew where he was or what
had happened to him. Some surmised that he had enlisted
in an Australian regiment in World War I and had perished
in battle, but a few years ago Pat was discovered in a small
town in northern California. He was brought on to Madi-

son for one of the home-coming games, and given a great welcome and ovation.

The president of the University was the scholarly Charles Kendall Adams, former president of Cornell, and author of important works in European history. He wore a divided beard and, because of some eye ailment, there was a droop to his eyelids. Always over his shoulders hung a black cape. Scholar and historian though he was, President Adams was singularly successful in handling the rustic members of the State Legislature and in securing from them large appropriations for the University.

Other notable personalities on the Wisconsin faculty were Stephen Moulton Babcock, Dean of the School of Agriculture and inventor of that boon to all farmers, the Babcock Milk Test. The farmers' sons came to the University for what was called the "short course" in the winter. When they came out from their classrooms, the other students would line the walks and greet them with lowing, baying, neighing, and cock-crowing. How foolish and thoughtless is youth! These "short horns" as we called them, represented the basic industry of human society. Yet we all jeered at them!

I was not in his classes, but I frequently saw the frail-looking Richard Theodore Ely, the famous economist, with a Philadelphia lawyer's green book bag under his arm as he walked down State Street. There had been a big commotion about his alleged socialistic teachings, and the declaration of academic freedom drawn up by the Regents of the University at that time, and now inscribed on the main building of the University. It was, no doubt, a good and timely utterance; but the puzzling question sometimes arises—how far ought academic freedom to go? Suppose a professor should advocate stealing, adultery, or murder; would it be an infringement of academic freedom to dismiss him?

Dr. Charles Richard Van Hise, afterwards president of the University, and one of America's foremost geologists, was my professor in that science. Around Madison there were good displays of glacial moraine, and on those fine autumn days Dr. Van Hise would take us out on field expeditions. In the early mornings, too, I used to walk along the shores of beautiful Lake Mendota and gather baskets of stones on the beach for classification. One thing I remember about Dr. Van Hise is that never in any way, in discussing the geological epochs, did he reflect upon the Bible record of the creation. Indeed, that was true of the University as a whole; and I have sometimes said that if I had a son I would send him to an altogether secular institution like the University of Wisconsin, where the Bible was not even mentioned, rather than to one of our ecclesiastical, or quasi-ecclesiastical colleges, where the Bible is taught, but always from the modernistic and rationalistic viewpoint. In that connection, I recall what a professor of history said one night when he was giving the usual criticism of the oration of a young man in one of the literary societies at the University of Denver. The student had spoken sneeringly of the account of the Creation in the Book of Genesis. In his comment Dr. James Edward Le Rossignol said: "When we speak of the Creation, it behooves us to be humble, for we must remember that none of us was present on that occasion." The wise man of the Book of Proverbs said, "A word spoken in season, how good it is." Through all the years since, that "word in season," spoken by that history professor, has remained with me. The abiding influence of a chance saying like that gives us faith in the spoken word, both public and private, and encourages us to "sow our seed in the morning, and in the evening withhold not our hand."

We had two professors of Greek, the aged Alexander "Zeus" Kerr, and the brilliant Charles Forster Smith. In

Latin I had Dr. Moses Stephen Slaughter. In 1925, as I was wandering through the beautiful Protestant Cemetery at Rome, just outside the walls of the city, and hard by the Pyramid of Cestius, near the site of St. Paul's martyrdom, I came suddenly upon the grave of my old professor of Latin at Wisconsin. As Tacitus wrote, "Every man should try to leave a happy memory of himself," and that Dr. Slaughter succeeded in doing.

Old Dr. John Barber Parkinson, one of the first professors at the University, had a rather soft course in that now almost-obsolete subject, International Law. This will show how "soft" the course was. Dr. Parkinson would say, when he reviewed a lecture and quizzed the class, "Once an Englishman always what, Macartney?" The history department was the strongest in the University. In American history there was Frederick Jackson Turner, and in medieval history, Charles Homer Haskins, afterwards dean of the graduate school at Harvard. He, more than any other teacher, brought out for me the romance of history. But perhaps the teacher who made the most lasting impressions on me and my brother was the professor of public speech, Dr. David Bower Frankenburgher. A genial, kindly soul, he encouraged us in good speaking and stirred our ambition. When I was at the University, the orator and the debater were as well known as the heroes of the gridiron. Among the noted orators and debaters in my day at Wisconsin were Joseph Harry Loeb, a brilliant Jew; Michael Olbrich, William Samuel Kies, and Joseph Edward Davies, in recent years Ambassador to Belgium and to Russia.

There were three debating halls: Athena, Hesperia, and Philomathia. Athena and Hesperia had their halls at opposite ends of the top story of Main Hall, and thither the ambitious orators and debaters resorted every Friday night. I joined the oldest and most renowned of the debating societies, Athena, with its sacred cock on the wall. On the twentieth anniversary of my pastorate in Pittsburgh, E. T. O'Brien, a fellow member of the debating society, sent this recollection to the church:

"You might be interested in an incident which happened in the Ancient Athenian Debating Society, during a debate. The question was, *Did the Teachings of Ingersoll Result in More Good than Harm?* Dr. Macartney was on the negative, and I was one of the affirmative debators. Our debate leader was Morgan, and in closing the debate, he made a violent, unfair and bitter attack on Christianity and especially on the teachings of Presbyterianism. Dr. Macartney was the last speaker, and as I looked at him, his face was aglow. When Morgan sat down, Dr. Macartney immediately took the glasses from his nose, jumped upon the table in the center of the room, and made the most brilliant and effective speech I have ever heard. It was a thrilling moment to see him on top of the secretary's table. He looked at the sixty-five members present, and opened by saying, 'I resent the insult that the speaker has levied on the Presbyterian Church. Most of my ancestors, from the time of Bobby Burns until now, were Presbyterian clergymen, and they were unselfish, indefatigable, scholarly, and useful members of the Christian Church.' His speech lasted about five minutes, and at the close, everybody cheered, and cheered, and cheered. Morgan had made a great mistake, and he realized it after hearing that speech."

I had forgotten about the table, but I remembered the ardor with which I had spoken. After all, our truly eloquent moments are when we are in dead earnest.

The annual joint debate was a great event. The debaters worked for a year on their debates, which were frequently published in book or pamphlet form. The winning argument on the Free Silver question in the joint debate of

1896, the year of "16 to 1," was published by the Republican National Committee as a campaign document.

In 1900 I represented the University of Wisconsin in the Northern Oratorical League, made up of Wisconsin, Michigan, Northwestern, Iowa, Illinois, Chicago, and Minnesota. The subject of my oration was "National Apostasy," and in it I dealt with the then much-discussed national trend towards imperialism, as shown by our holding the Philippine Islands. That was the chief issue of the 1900 presidential campaign, McKinley against Bryan. The first time I saw or heard William Jennings Bryan was in that campaign when he spoke at the Monona Lake Chautauqua Grounds. What a splendid figure he was then, still in his thirties; the picture of physical vigor; and that magnificent voice, with no loud-speakers to magnify it, heard in all its bell-like resonance by the thousands.

In after years I was to see much of Mr. Bryan. In the great theological controversies in the Presbyterian Church, 1923-1925, over the Christ-dishonoring doctrines of modernism, Mr. Bryan made the nominating speech at Grand Rapids when I was elected Moderator of the General Assembly. I was driving with him in the winter of that year through Chicago in a taxi on our way to the McCormick Theological Seminary, where we were both to speak. On the way we passed the auditorium where the Democratic Convention of 1896 met. This was where Mr. Bryan made the great speech which resulted in his nomination for the Presidency, and which ended with the celebrated peroration, "You shall not press down upon the brow of labor this crown of thorns; you shall not crucify mankind upon a cross of gold." As we drove past the auditorium I said to him, "Mr. Bryan, many times before that convention, no doubt, you must have made just as good a speech, which was never heard of."

"Yes," he replied, "I suppose that is true; but that Convention was my opportunity, and I made the most of it." He was silent for a little, as the look of reminiscence came into his eyes as his great head rested against the cushion of the taxicab. Then he added, "And that's about all we do in this life—use or lose our opportunity."

I have always considered it a happy and fortunate thing that I had somewhat close personal relationship with two of America's greatest orators and political figures. I have already spoken of one of them, Mr. Bryan. The other was Robert M. LaFollette. The LaFollette home was a block below ours on Wilson Street. I used to see the two boys, the future Governor and Senator, Philip and Robert, playing football on the lawn of their home, and the daughter, Fola, was in one of my classes at the University. Among college orators, Bob LaFollette was famous as the only Wisconsin man who had won the contest in the Northern Oratorical League. That was back in 1879. His oration was a masterly study of Shakespeare's "Iago." I remember the day I picked up in the library of Wisconsin a collection of the winning orations in the Northern Oratorical League. There I read LaFollette's "Iago," and also a beautiful oration by John Finley, of Knox College, on John Brown. It commenced with a description of John Brown's lonely grave in the Adirondack mountains. Thirty-five years afterwards, I spoke at a banquet in the interests of the National Presbyterian Church at Washington. One of the other speakers was Dr. John Finley, then editor of "The New York Times," and in my speech I turned aside to say to him, and the others, how much I owed to that oration of his on John Brown. Among other things, it taught me how effective a description or historical anecdote can be at the beginning of a speech.

LaFollette had marked histrionic ability, and was am-

bitious to be an actor; but the story was that he had consulted the American tragedian, McCullough, who told him
that he was too short of stature to be a success on the stage.
But whether on the stage or not, LaFollette was certainly an
actor on the political platform. He illustrated Demosthenes'
definition of successful oratory, "Action! Action! Action!"

Called "Half-breeds," LaFollette and his followers had
been hammering away for years at the Republican machine
in Wisconsin, led by able men such as Senator Philetus Saw-
yer, Senator Spooner, and Governor Schofield. LaFollette
had served three terms in Congress, but had not yet
succeeded in his efforts to get the nomination for the governorship. Because of his renown as a university orator, I asked
him to coach me in the delivery of my oration as the representative of Wisconsin in the Northern Oratorical League
Contest of that year. He was busily engaged in his law practice, and was also in the midst of a political campaign.
Nevertheless, he gladly assented to help me, and in the
later afternoons, when court had adjourned, he put me
through my paces in the court room of the Dane County
Court House. The contest was held that year in Library
Hall at Wisconsin. One of the contestants representing
Michigan was George Maxey, who delivered an able oration
on Daniel Webster. Maxey later became Chief Justice of the
Supreme Court of Pennsylvania. First prize was won by the
orator from Northwestern University, who gave a certainly
vivid description and fervent denunciation of the lynching
of a Negro. I was given second place, and would have won
first place easily but for the fact that one of the judges on
manuscript gave me sixth place. The day after the contest
I met LaFollette in front of the Capitol at Madison. He
stopped me and said he had read the account of the contest
on the train that morning. Then, looking earnestly at me,
and turning his head to one side in a characteristic posture,

and pointing his forefinger at me, he said, "Macartney, the man who gave you sixth place was either a knave or a fool." *

My oration on National Apostasy began with a description of the empty niche in the monument on the battlefield of Saratoga, the niche where should have stood the statue of the hero of that field, Benedict Arnold, an honor forfeited by his subsequent treason. At the fortieth reunion of my class in Wisconsin, one of my classmates came over to my chair and said, "On the battlefield of Saratoga there stands a towering obelisk, commemorative of that decisive struggle of the Revolution. About the base of the monument are four niches, in which are the statues of the generals who commanded on that field. In the first, stands Horatio Gates; in the second, Schuyler; in the third, Morgan; but the fourth, alas! stand empty." So he went on through the introduction of my oration, word for word. Another told me that he had heard a man get it off at a Rotary or Kiwanis Club. He

---

* Editor's note: How keenly Dr. Macartney felt that defeat may be seen in the letter he sent to his parents after the contest:

Madison, Wisconsin,
May 13th, 1900

Dear Father and Mother:

The battle is over; the wounded have been taken to the rear; the dead are buried. The Grand Guard has made its last stand. Waterloo has been fought and won! But the victory should have been mine. Already I had despatched a courier to Paris, telling of victory. But alas! Blücher appeared in the person of a judge from Indiana. Even then, I had hopes of victory. I ordered Ney's horse to charge, but my splendid squadrons went down to death on the sunken road of Ohain. So here I sit on my island rock, fighting the battle over again, and wondering why it rained, and why I overlooked the sunken road.

After my long campaign I am slowly getting used to the civilian life, and am gathering up the loose ends of my studies. The papers will tell you all about the different contests. It has been a long, hard strain, but the benefits derived are great.

said he was inclined to go up and tell the speaker how he had heard what he had said forty years ago, but he was generous enough to refrain from so doing. One of the professors at Lincoln University told me once how, at an oratorical contest, the orator who won the prize had stirred them all with the speech he delivered. But when he went home, the professor thought that there was something familiar about the oration, especially the introduction, with the description of the monument on the battlefield at Saratoga. He turned to his shelves in his library, picked up the volume of "Winning Orations," a collection of first-and second-place orations in the Northern Oratorical League, and soon came upon my oration on "National Apostasy." The fellow had delivered my oration verbatim. That has happened, too, with some of my sermons. I have never objected, because imitation is said to be the highest form of praise.

The last time I heard LaFollette was on the stump at Paterson, New Jersey, in one of his unsuccessful efforts for the Republican nomination for the Presidency. In 1924 he ran as an Independent on the Progressive ticket against Coolidge, the Republican nominee, and John W. Davis, the Democratic, and received almost 5,000,000 votes, the largest vote ever given to a third-party candidate. LaFollette was looked upon thirty years ago, and even before that, as a radical, and a dangerous man. Today, many of the things which he advocated have become the accepted law of the land, and no one advocates their repeal. LaFollette often spoke of his friend and teacher, Wisconsin's philosopher-president, John Bascom. When LaFollette was in the midst of his campaigns, Bascom wrote him, "Robert, you can afford to make political mistakes, but you can never afford to be wrong." In World War I, an unsuccessful effort was made to oust LaFollette from the Senate. The moral courage and independence of LaFollette is to be measured by the fact that he alone in the Senate objected to immediate consideration of the War Resolution putting the United States in World War I, and was one of six Senators who voted against the Resolution.

Before I took the job on the ranch near Morrison, when I was a freshman at the University of Denver, I applied for work at the ranch of Levi Booth, on Cherry Creek, near Denver. The old gentleman was reading the newspaper in his living room at the ranch as I talked with him through the screened window. He asked me if I could drive a team. I had never driven a team, but since I had driven the family horse, I thought I could drive two horses as well as one, and told him so. He then said I could have the job and told me to report the next day. But instead of going there, I took the job at the Morrison ranch. That fall, when I entered the University of Wisconsin, I picked up one evening the "Daily Cardinal," the college paper, and the first thing I saw was this headline: "Levi Booth, first graduate of the University of Wisconsin, gored by a bull on his ranch near Denver." It was the very man to whom I had applied for a job. Thus, in a sense, I saw the beginning of the University of Wisconsin.

CHAPTER XI

A YEAR OUT

When I say, "a year out," I do not mean that it was an unimportant or an unprofitable year. Indeed, it was a very profitable year; but it was "a year out" in the sense that it was a break in my formal schooling and education. After my graduation from the University of Wisconsin, I returned to our family home, Fern Cliffe, at Beaver Falls, Pennsylvania, it having been opened again after the return of my father and mother from Scotland. What was to be my next step? I had specialized in English at Wisconsin, and, still uncertain as to my work in life, set out for Harvard, armed with a letter of introduction and commendation from my English professor at Wisconsin to the famed Barrett Wendell. I took lodgings with a Beaver Falls schoolmate, Henry George, son of the president of Geneva College, and himself, afterwards, president of the same college. But the spirit of unrest was upon me, and having a little money which I had won in the oratorical contest, I forsook Harvard before I heard any lectures, and sailed on the steamship *Winifredian,* bound for Liverpool. I spent a few days in Glasgow with one of my Scottish uncles, and visited Rothesay, on the Isle of Bute, my mother's birthplace, Blairbeth, her beautiful home near Glasgow, and other places associated with the Robertson family. Then I departed for Edinburgh, with the thought of studying there for a degree. I had an interview with the noted critic, Professor G. E. B. Saintsbury, and attended one of his lectures. But still the fever of unrest was upon me, and I left Edinburgh for London. I can hear now the never-ceasing, all-night rumble and roar of the omnibuses as they passed my hotel that first night.

In London I visited all the chief places of interest, and on a November afternoon saw the Lord Mayor's show. Leaving London, I went down to Whitehaven, and took ship for France, landing at Dieppe, forty-one years later to be the scene of the first Allied landing and exploratory landing by Canadian troops in World War II. Paris in those November days seemed to me rather dull and flat. Innocence and inexperience sometimes will be a danger, but sometimes also a shield of defense. I was sitting on a bench in one of the parks, when a very pretty and stylishly dressed young woman came up and accosted me, asking, apparently, some question. I shook my head, and in the little French I could command, I told her I did not understand what she was saying. She stood for a little, and then, with a pretty smile, half amusement, half pity, left me. After she was gone I began to understand what she wanted. Only three times, I think, in my life, and in all my travels, has such a thing happened; this time in Paris, once on Michigan Avenue in Chicago, and once on the waterfront at Beirut, Syria.

In Paris it was Napoleon's tomb that impressed me most of all, as I looked down upon the red granite coffin of the great conqueror, with the sunlight pouring through the golden windows as if to reflect the effulgence of eternal fame. The battle flags surround the tomb, and on the

pillars are inscribed the names of his great victories: Jena,
Wagram, Marengo, Austerlitz, and all the rest. In London
it was Westminster Abbey that stirred me more than anything else; and in Scotland, the Wallace monument at Stir-
ling, where I saw the mighty two-edged sword of that Scottish
patriot. Bannockburn, where Robert Bruce defeated King
Edward's army, whetted my military and historical inclination. My mother's clan, the Robertsons, fought at Bannockburn under Bruce, from whom the Robertson clan takes its
name.

I returned to America late in the year, landing in Philadelphia, and went up to Princeton to visit my brother Albert, who was in the Theological Seminary. I had an interview, too, with Dean West about entering the graduate school
of the University, and then returned to Beaver Falls.* In the

* Editor's note: The uncertainty in Dr. Macartney's mind during
this period is reflected in a letter he sent to his sister:

Beaver Falls, Pa.,
Feb. 7, 1902.

My dear Mina:

There will be no peace in the house until I satisfy mother that I
have written you a letter; so I suppose I might as well acquiesce in
the matter. But I have really nothing to tell you. As for myself, I
arise about nine in the morning, have my breakfast, and after breakfast
my newspaper. After that comes a trip to the post office, or, perhaps,
a little shoveling of snow up to the dormitory and back. The rest of
the time is taken up with a little reading, a little writing, and a great
deal of swearing. So runs my little world away! Not very startling, you
think?

Your Teachers' agencies are good for nothing. I received notice
of a vacancy from each of the Agencies, but in neither case was I successful in my application. I have been endeavoring to get onto the
staff of several newspapers, and have had equally gratifying success in
this field also. It looks as if I should have to fall into the clerical rut
also. I am thinking of going into the Army—fine, exciting life, that!
Nothing further.

Clarence

[The family evidently was concerned about his plans, and his brother Robertson, already a minister for some years, wrote at that time:]

First Presbyterian Church
Oconto, Wisconsin,
February 9th, 1902

My dear Clarence:

Do you want to know how a minister puts in his day? This is a Sabbath evening and it has been a blessed day in my heart and in the church. Well, I will commence and give you a "Sabbath Day's Journey." I got up a little after seven and took a cold plunge, gargled my nose and throat with salt water, brushed my teeth, and shaved and dressed. Breakfast is ready at 7:30. Then I go to the church and have my own private devotions which on Sabbath are extra heavy. Nothing prepares for the pulpit and for the success and work of the day like a season of communion and prayer with the Manager whose work we are trying to accomplish. Before Church time at ten-thirty I usually have a consultation with the Janitor and the Choir Leader. Then for five minutes before the service I am on my knees, and when the organ prelude strikes up I go by the side door to the pulpit. It is always with a light heart; I am happiest there. Feel like flying in the air.

*   *   *

I had a good audience of many strangers and many men. More and more men are coming out. We have a Christian engineer recently come to town, and tonight he had his fireman and four other railroad men with him. God blessed the sermon and the service, and I am asking him that some soul may have been saved and some drifter arrested and brought to moorings. Now I am going home. I just thought you might like to know how I put in the day. I am always as fresh as when I get out of bed in the morning, and never a bit nervous. May God bless you, my dear brother, and guide you in this trying time of uncertainty as to your life work. Do not worry and do not grow anxious. In years to come it will all seem wonderful in the way you have been led and guided. The only life that makes no mistakes is the Life of Faith and prayer and the life with Christ, and even the mistakes are overruled for our good. ✔

With much love to you all. Good night.

Your loving brother,
Robertson

117

spring of that year I took a post as a reporter on the county paper, the "Beaver Times." This turned out to be a most important chapter in my training for the work of my life. I had a taste for composition, and my work on the "Times" gave ample scope for the cultivation of that taste and whatever talent I may have had in that line. One of my duties was to report the proceedings in the Criminal Court. There I saw much that was of a nature to uphold the fundamental Christian doctrine of the Fall of man. In his *Back to Methuselah,* George Bernard Shaw makes one of his characters say to a man who questions the doctrine of the Fall: "With that picture before you, will you now ask me where was the Fall? You might as well stand at the foot of a Snowden [a mountain in Wales] and ask me, 'Where is the mountain?'" Yes, if anyone doubts the truth of the Christian doctrine of the Fall of man, I suggest that he sit out a few sessions of the Criminal Court.

Newspaper reporting taught me to be clear and lucid in what I wrote, and also that the drama of human life is always interesting. If in any way my pulpit preaching and my writings have been clear or interesting, I owe much of that to my newspaper experience. I wrote also the heads for the paper. One morning we got a rather garbled account of a scuffle between a "Squire," or Justice of the Peace, and a lad in Bridgewater. The boy with others had been trespassing in the squire's cornfield, and in the scuffle which ensued, quite by accident, the tong of the squire's fork, which he was holding, pierced the boy's hand. I ran a head halfway across the front page of the paper: "Ran him through with a pitchfork!" I still think it was a good head. But the paper was hardly on the street when the telephone began to ring, and we had a very irate squire on our hands. With another from the office, I went down to the squire's plantation and walked the field with him, and so managed to placate him.

CHAPTER XII

PRINCETON

GOING recently through some of my mother's letters, I came upon a letter which she had written to my brother Robertson at the time I was working on the "Beaver Times" and was still a little uncertain as to the next step. In the letter she said, "I never knew anyone who was so clearly marked for the pulpit as Clarence, if only the Lord would put grace in his heart."

My father and three brothers were all in the ministry before me. I had some inclination toward a college post as a teacher of English or history, and thought a little about the law, too. But, as the present narrative indicates, I was destined for the pulpit. At the end of my summer's work on the newspaper I went down to New Haven and matriculated in the Yale Divinity School. Why Yale? Partly, perhaps, because my brother was already at Princeton and partly because of a degree of something akin to revolt against the orthodox position, a state of mind not uncommon in men just out of college. The subject of my thesis for the bachelor's degree at Wisconsin had been, "A comparative analysis of Byron's 'Cain' and Shelly's 'Prometheus Unbound.'" The magnificent lines of revolt in those two poems naturally made something of an appeal to me. Yale seemed a little removed from the orthodox position, yet not altogether heterodox. But my stay at Yale was very brief. I attended, I think, just one class, the class in Hebrew, and very ably taught by a noted Old Testament scholar, and then packed my bag and retreated to Princeton, where I entered the junior class of the Theological Seminary. Looking back today over that year of indecision and restlessness—Harvard, Edinburgh, Paris, the "Beaver Times," Yale, and finally Princeton—I firmly believe that the hand of the Lord was leading me and guarding me when I knew it not. Princeton Theological Seminary, with its grand and ancient tradition of a stalwart defense of the truth, and of the glory of the Christian revelation, was the right thing for me. I had found my true place. Henceforth, there was no wavering; no halting between two opinions, but straight forward towards the goal.

When I was in Scotland the winter before, my uncle introduced me on High Street in Edinburgh to Principal Robert Rainy, who had been a leading spirit in the merger of the United Presbyterian Church and the Free Church. My uncle said something to him about my being uncertain as to the next step and my work in life. Principal Rainy put his hand on my shoulder and, looking kindly down upon me from his great height, said, quoting the verse in the Book of Proverbs, "In all thy ways acknowledge him, and he shall direct thy paths." I have never doubted for a moment that it was the hand of the Lord that led me past the gates of Harvard, Yale, Edinburgh, the newspaper office, and the professor's chair to the halls of Princeton Seminary. "There is a divinity that shapes our ends."

I was assigned a room on the first floor of Brown Hall; became a member of the Friars Club, and thus began my life at Princeton Seminary. Contrary to popular thought, Princeton Seminary has never had any formal connection with

Princeton University. Yet, until recent years, there was always a close tie between the two institutions. The Seminary was founded in 1812, and its first two professors were the noted Archibald Alexander and Samuel Miller. Afterwards, the celebrated theologian, Charles Hodge, joined the faculty. Princeton has a noble tradition of loyalty to the Christian faith. At the Centennial celebration of the Seminary, I heard Dr. Francis Landey Patton, the then president, say that when the archaeologists of future ages unearthed the remains of Princeton Seminary, they would at least agree that it belonged to the order of vertebrates. Perhaps that could have been said then, at the 100th anniversary of the Seminary, with more conviction than today; yet still, as theological seminaries go, Princeton stands pretty well up in the order of vertebrates.

Shortly after I enrolled in the Seminary, Woodrow Wilson, who had been nominated for the post of his predecessor, Dr. Patton, was inaugurated as president of Princeton University. It was at that celebration that I first saw the ex-President of the United States, Grover Cleveland, who had purchased a home in Bayard Lane. Mrs. Cleveland was then still a comparatively young and very beautiful woman. The boys from the Seminary who attended the service at the First Church always looked with interest upon her as she came down the aisle to her pew. Grover Cleveland was the son of a Presbyterian minister, and had great reverence for the Church and for Christianity, but he never made a public profession of his faith in Christ. Perhaps one reason was the unfortunate departure from the moral code which was brought out in the campaign when he ran against James G. Blaine in 1884. Like Andrew Jackson, Cleveland hesitated to unite with the church, lest the cry "hypocrite" should go up. But unlike Jackson, who when he had retired from the Presidency, kept the vow he had made to his beloved Rachel, and united with the Presbyterian church just across the road from the Hermitage, Cleveland in his retirement neither united with nor attended the church. Yet he frequently made mention of the debt he owed to his Presbyterian minister-father, and when he was dying at Princeton had the family send for the old hymn book out of which they used to sing at family worship when he was a boy in his father's home. Thus, to the music of those old hymns, the soul of Grover Cleveland passed into the unseen.

I did not attend Woodrow Wilson's classes in American History at the University, as did so many of the Seminary students, but I frequently heard him when he presided at the chapel services, and once at Murray-Dodge Hall I heard him deliver a searching sermon on the power and importance of a right inner-life, basing his remarks on the words of Jesus as related in St. Matthew's Gospel: "Do not ye yet understand that whatsoever entereth in at the mouth goeth into the belly, and is cast out into the draught? But those things which proceed out of the mouth come forth from the heart; and they defile the man. For out of the heart proceed evil thoughts, murders, adulteries, fornications, thefts, false witness, blasphemies. These are the things which defile a man."

Wilson was a guest one night at the Friars Club when I had some conversation with him. Speaking of Dr. Patton, he said he was "the ablest man on his feet" he had ever heard, meaning that Dr. Patton could make a better extemporaneous speech than any other man. Once when Dr. Patton was delivering his lectures on "Fundamental Christianity" in Philadelphia, I told him what Woodrow Wilson had said of his ability as an extemporaneous orator. "Umph," ejaculated Dr. Patton, "That's the first time I ever heard Wilson say anything good of me." When Dr. Patton suddenly resigned as President of Princeton University, he at the same time nominated to the Trustees, Woodrow Wilson as his successor; whereupon Wilson was elected, despite the fact that had there been longer consideration, Henry Van Dyke, who had many supporters for the post, might have been chosen. Dr. Patton always deeply resented the fact that in his inaugural address Wilson never adverted to him or his successful administration of the University. As events turned out, when Patton that day in the trustees' meeting nominated Wilson as his successor, he was, in reality, naming Wilson as President of the United States, for, unless he had been President of Princeton, Wilson would not have been elected as Governor of New Jersey; and except for his record as Governor of New Jersey, he would not have been nominated by the Democratic party for the Presidency of the United States. Thus do great issues turn on the hinges of apparently small events.

In that same conversation with Wilson at the Friars Club I heard him say of Henry Van Dyke, quoting, I think, what someone else had said, that Van Dyke was the only man he had ever known who could "strut sitting down." When we got on the subject of religion and the church, Wilson said that for him the whole truth of Christianity rested upon the truth of the complete deity of Jesus Christ. If Christ were not the Son of God, then, he declared, there was no Christianity. One of my first books, *The Minister's Son*, I dedicated to Woodrow Wilson, and he wrote me a gracious note concerning the introductory paragraph in which I spoke of his father, the Reverend Dr. Joseph Wilson. On one of my Civil War expeditions I stopped at the home of Dr. James R. Graham, the minister emeritus of the Presbyterian Church in Winchester, Virginia. It was in Dr. Graham's home that Stonewall Jackson had his headquarters when he was in command in the Valley of Virginia. He told me many interesting anecdotes of that great soldier, and said that, first and foremost, above all else, Jackson was an earnest Christian. Dr. Graham said he had known many of the great men of his day, before, during, and after the Civil War, but, looking back, he considered that the greatest of them all was the Reverend Dr. Joseph Wilson, the father of Woodrow Wilson.

There were some remarkable personalities on the Seminary faculty in my day. One was Dr. John DeWitt, professor of Church History. He was not equipped in a technical sense as are most professors in that field, but he had something that technical research cannot bestow, and gave us most interesting lectures on the great epochs and the commanding personalities of church history. He was a short, rather pompous man, and wore the first brown derby that I had ever seen, a type of head-gear made famous by Al Smith in his 1928 campaign for the presidency. Once when we had assembled for prayers in Stuart Hall, it was Dr. DeWitt's time to conduct the devotions. When he came on the platform, he stepped forward to the reading desk, opened the Bible to the passage he was going to read, selected a hymn, and then, without turning, stepped backward in his stately way and sat down on the center chair. Unfortunately, Robert, the janitor, had removed the seat of the chair for repair and had spread a cloth over the opening. Dr. DeWitt went clear through, doubling up like a jackknife, while Dr. Greene on one side, and Dr. Patton on the other, peering down through his thick glasses, sought to extricate him. Had it been anyone else save the pompous Dr. DeWitt, it would not have been so funny. Dr. DeWitt's assistant, and afterwards his successor, the scholarly and brilliant Dr. Loetscher, did more than any other to open for me the thrill, romance and majesty of the long history of the Christian Church. This proved to be of the highest importance for me in my work as a minister.

The professor of Systematic Theology was Dr. Benjamin Breckenridge Warfield, of the famous Breckenridge family of Kentucky. (In addition to his accomplishments as a theologian, Dr. Warfield, with his brother Ethelbert, then president of Lafayette College, had written an autoritative book on the cow.) His wife was an invalid, injured, they said, by a fall when on their honeymoon in Switzerland. She never appeared in public; but I used to see her as, clad in a blue veil, she walked to and fro with her husband on the back gallery of their home.

In the Old Testament we had the renowned Robert Dick Wilson. He was noted for his asides, such as telling us one day that a man should never marry a woman unless he was willing to go to hell for her sake. The president of the Seminary and the first president it ever had, was Dr. Francis Landey Patton, formerly president of Princeton University. Dr. Patton, a native of Bermuda, and who never renounced his British citizenship, was an early graduate of the Seminary, and had served three churches before becoming a professor at the McCormick Theological Seminary in Chicago. It was while in Chicago that he achieved national fame as the chief prosecutor in the heresy trial of David Swing, the poetic and gifted minister of the Fourth Presbyterian Church. From McCormick, Dr. Patton came to Princeton Seminary as professor of Apologetics, and was then elected president of the University. Upon his resignation, he was called back to the Seminary as its president. He was a *laissez faire* sort of administrator, and when president of the University conducted its affairs without even a secretary. Very near-sighted, he never knew a student, and it was said could not recognize his own wife when he met her on the street. In urging men to read widely and systematically, he remarked, somewhat facetiously, of course, how his own regular reading, going through such works as Gibbon's *Decline and Fall of the Roman Empire*, had ruined three churches, but had made him.

While president of the University he was always voted by the students their favorite preacher. As he preached he would keep toying with his handkerchief, always turning his head far to the right. Once when he was delivering his lectures in Philadelphia, standing in a pulpit clear over on one side of the church, and turning to the right as usual, I mustered up the courage to tell him that if he turned more to the left, he would be better heard by the congregation. He could rise to greater heights than any preacher I have ever heard; but he could also, according to his mood, and the degree of his preparation, sink to a very low level. Once I met him on his way to Miller Chapel on a Commencement occasion, and he said to me that he was trying to "scratch the surface of his brain" for some appropriate idea. A characteristic Patton saying was his injunction to the departing class, "Pray without ceasing, and shave every day!" He had certain quotations, especially from Tennyson's "In Memoriam," which he made use of in almost every sermon he preached.

On my second vacation I went to Bermuda. When the ship was warped into its berth, I saw Dr. Patton standing on the dock, and made myself known to him. He was generous enough to invite me to preach for him in the Warwick Scottish Church. I, of course, was not foolish enough to accept the invitation; but on the Sabbath afternoon I went over to Warwick and heard him preach. The gallery was filled with Negroes, and the white people sat in the body of the church. In his sermon Dr. Patton used the same theological and scholarly terms which he used at Princeton, yet he held the attention of everybody, the blacks as well as the whites. His text was "Let us hear the conclusion of the whole matter," and he certainly went everywhere preaching the gospel! At length he came to the subject of immortality. Lifting his right arm, and marking off a line on the pillar alongside him, he quoted the verse from the 23rd Psalm, "Yea though I walk through the valley of the shadow of death, I will fear no evil, for Thou art with me." "There," said Dr. Patton, "is the high water mark of Old Testament faith in the future life—willing to go, but wanting to stay." Then, marking a still higher line on the stone pillar, he quoted the words of St. Paul in the Epistle to the Philippians, "For I am in a strait betwixt two, having a desire to depart and be with Christ; which is far better: nevertheless to abide in the flesh is more needful for you." "There," said Dr. Patton, "is the high water mark of New Testament faith in the future life—willing to stay, but wanting to go."

CHAPTER XIII

A WISCONSIN VILLAGE

MY first sermon was preached in a little pine church in the woods at Tuckahoe, New Jersey, not far from Ocean City. A young man's first sermon is always, for him at least, a memorable occasion. Because preaching a sermon can be compared with nothing else in the world, there is something tender, deeply moving, about the minister's first sermon. I had at least a good text from the 12th chapter of St. John's Gospel: "Except a corn of wheat fall into the ground and die, it abideth alone." In the sermon I used an illustration from George Eliot's *Silas Marner*, how when the lonely Silas, embittered because his gold had been stolen, found one night the golden-haired little girl, whose mother had perished in the snowstorm, lying on the floor of his cabin, and took the child into his home and into his heart to care for her and bring her up, he died unto himself, and thus entered the gates of a new life.

At the end of my first year in the Seminary I received an invitation to supply the pulpit of the Presbyterian Church at Prairie du Sac, Wisconsin. There had been an unhappy division in the congregation over the last ministry, and the two sides were somewhat bitter one against the other. I was commended to the clerk of session by the minister of the Presbyterian church at Madison, who had known me when I was a student at the University of Wisconsin. I suppose he had recommended me because he knew something of me and my background, and was familiar with the part I had taken in public speech and oratory at the University. But that was not it. He wrote me that he had commended me to the divided church because "I knew enough to keep my mouth shut." And that certainly I did, so far as the church quarrel was concerned.

When I got off the St. Paul train at the little station, Elder Conway Moore, a fine silver-haired gentleman from New Jersey, met me and conducted me to the home where I was to get my meals. Elder Moore lived in the toll house at the bridge over the Wisconsin. I was often in that home for dinner, with the Wisconsin flowing rapidly away underneath the dining room. The memory of Mrs. Moore's gooseberry jam abides with me to this day. When I arrived, the town was under the shadow of the recent drowning in the river of two fine young people, members of the senior class at the high school. I had, as I remember, just two sermons, one on Judas, and one on "Except a corn of wheat," and had to preach twice the first Sabbath. Dr. David J. Burrell, then at the zenith of his fame as minister of the Marble Collegiate Church, Fifth Avenue, New York, used to come down to Princeton every Monday and lecture to us in homiletics and hear us preach our class sermons. Two things he sank into us: first, a clear outline; second, to preach without notes. That first Sabbath at Prairie du Sac I knew my sermon thoroughly; yet I took the manuscript with me into the pulpit, and although I never referred to it, the very fact that it was there seemed to chain me to the pulpit. I resolved to try it without a manuscript. The next Sabbath, and through all the Sabbaths of the many years since then, I have never taken a manuscript or notes of any kind into the pulpit. One of my first sermons at Prairie du Sac was on the text, "Felix trembled." Sitting just in front of me, but unknown to me, was a man whose name was Felix, and who, some of the congregation said, had good reason to tremble.

In the back of the church just over the doorway was a little two-by-four gallery. One night that gallery was filled. Perhaps that little gallery, filled with say fifteen or twenty people, and among them the postmaster, who had quit the church in a huff when the last minister departed, brought me more joy than the crowded galleries of my three churches where I have served as minister: the First Church of Paterson, New Jersey; the Arch Street Church, Philadelphia, and the First Presbyterian Church, Pittsburgh.

Before I came that summer, one of the Session had remarked that by getting a young man from the Seminary for a few months at $50.00 per month, they could save considerable money. Just back of the manse where I slept and studied, there lived a singular old pioneer, Thomas Payne. He had been a farmer on the prairie and a cattle drover. It was said that he would feed his cattle salt, and then on the way to the market drive them through the Wisconsin, where they drank copiously, thus adding many pounds to their weight. Payne had been an adherent of the departed minister, and, like many others, had quit the sanctuary. He had heard of how they were going to save some money by getting a youth from the Seminary, and meeting Mr. Moore, the Clerk of Session, one morning said to him, "Elder Moore, when's that Cheap John preacher of yourn comin'?" One morning Payne stuck his head and long beard through the window of my study and greeted me. That was the beginning of a warm friendship. At every service he and his wife were there in the front row, listening eagerly to their "Cheap John preacher." He told me many interesting, and sometimes extraordinary, tales of the early days on the Wisconsin and on the Prairie.

There were many well-educated persons in the congregation. One, Professor Oscar Atwood, was the president of a Congregational college for Negroes in New Orleans. A frequent companion on my walks over the hills was a Harvard student, Louis Cooper, on the editorial board of the Harvard "Lampoon," the college paper. We had a real choir, and a soprano with a voice as sweet as any I have ever heard since, even in the highly paid choirs of my three churches. The pretty little village was a bit of Vermont, set down on the banks of the Wisconsin River. There I made my first sick calls; conducted my first funeral; delivered my first public address, a Fourth of July oration, in the grove on the bluffs. I preached twice every Sunday, and therefore had to study hard every day if I was to bring "well beaten oil" into the sanctuary. How I toiled during those hot July and August days, making sermonic "bricks without straw," that is, the straw of experience and wide study and reading. Now and then my neighbor, Payne, would look compassionately through the open window, where the bees were humming in the lilac bush, and say, "Elder (a New York name for preacher), are you still at it?" I had only a few books with me, and there was no library in the town. My own stock of sketches and illustrations was quickly exhausted, and, had it not been for the Old Testament characters, I would have gone into pulpit bankruptcy. But Joseph, Abraham, Jacob, David, Solomon, Samuel, Saul, Ruth, and the rest of them, saved the day for me. That experience taught me the appeal of biographical preaching, and thus opened for me a rich pulpit vein which I am still working.

The second summer I was invited to stay in the chief mansion of the town, a splendid brick house, with a lawn running down to the river. I remember that in my bedroom there were highly ornate and richly stitched shams, the old-time coverings for the pillows, fastened to the head of the bed, and let down during the day.

Across the river was the Kehl place, a handsome stone house looking over the river. Just adjoining it was a huge, but now abandoned, winery. There was a bright-eyed, dark-haired daughter in the family, Barbara, with whom now and then I used to roam the hills. She was later the wife of a Philadelphia minister, George B. Pence. The battle of Wisconsin Heights in the Black Hawk War had been fought near Prairie du Sac, and a mile up the river was a lofty crag known as Black Hawk. Frequently on the long summer evenings I would climb to that crag where Black Hawk, mounted on his white pony, had watched his followers in battle; and there, seated on a rock, with the Wisconsin flowing swiftly away towards the Mississippi, like the river of a man's life, I would think about my work and calling, and what the future held in store for me.

During my stay at Prairie du Sac, a young man, a classmate at the University, who lived on a farm over in Dane County, was drowned when bathing in the river. The Wisconsin is a noble river, one of the rivers by which Joliet and Marquette made their journey of exploration from the Great Lakes to the Mississippi. On my first vacation, when I commenced my ministry at Paterson, New Jersey, I went back to Prairie du Sac and followed in the footsteps of those French voyageurs, floating down the river by sunlight and moonlight in a pearl fisherman's barge, as far as Prairie du Chien on the Mississippi. In my first summer at Prairie du Sac, I was surprised that hardly anyone ever went swimming in the river. Once or twice I tried it by myself, but soon gave it up. The shadow of the many drownings seemed to hang over the river and warn off boaters and bathers. Where the river seemed to be placid and calm, it was, in reality, rushing toward the Mississippi with a rapidity and force of current against which the strongest swimmer could not contend. Its sand bars, which seemed to tell of a gradually declining beach, suddenly broke off into bottomless pools. Sometimes, in my sermons since that summer, I have used the Wisconsin River to illustrate the enticements and perils of temptation.

In that little riverside village those two summers, I had an invaluable preparation for the work of the ministry. There I came in close touch with the joys, the trials, the sorrows, and the beautiful affections of the common people. There I heard, and have never forgotten, the deep, glad, sad, sweet music of the human heart. One of the homes I liked to visit was that of Mr. J. Stephens Tripp, another Vermonter, straight as an arrow, who sat before me every Sunday in the first row of pews. He was the president of the local bank, and at the time of his death had amassed a large fortune, most of which he left to the University of Wisconsin. Tripp Hall, at the University, bears his name. When I went down to his bank at the end of the first summer to get my salary, $100 for the two months, Mr. Tripp handed me a check for just twice that amount. I looked at it and remarked, "There must be some mistake." "No," Mr. Tripp said, "we are giving you just twice the amount agreed upon as a token of our appreciation of your service." That $200, not in amount but in meaning, was the highest salary I have ever received. God bless the memory of those kind folk of that Wisconsin village, who thus encouraged the young minister with their appreciation, and strengthened his hand in the Lord. I spent a second summer among them, strengthening the ties formed in the first summer.

In my senior year at the Seminary, returning from a winter vacation spent at Prairie du Sac, I found under my door in Hodge Hall a letter from the Clerk of Session of the First Presbyterian Church of Paterson, New Jersey, inviting me to go down and preach a Sunday in their vacant pulpit. One of the Session had written a friend on the faculty asking him to suggest two likely men from the Senior class. The other man named was Lucian Lamar Knight. Knight was an associate of Henry Grady on the "Atlanta Constitution," when he felt an urge to enter the ministry, and came to the Seminary at Princeton. It was fourteen years since he had finished at the University of Georgia, and he was beyond the rest of us in years and experience. Because he came from the South, we called him "Colonel." He carried a gold-headed cane, wore a blue cut-away coat and white felt hat; but no one ever laughed at him, for all recognized his extraordinary talent. In the alphabetical order of names, he preached just before me in our class sermons in Miller Chapel. When he had finished his sermon, the critic, Dr. David J. Burrell of New York, turned to the class, saying: "Gentlemen, that is the way to preach," and called up the next preacher. Because of an unfortunate marriage, Knight demitted the ministry soon after he left the Seminary, and became the State Historian of Georgia.

Some years ago, driving down the Georgia coast on my way to Florida, I saw a sign indicating a road to St. Simon's Island. Remembering that in St. John's churchyard on that island there was the Oak under which John Wesley had preached, I resolved to turn aside and stand under that tree. Leaving my car at the gate of the churchyard, I entered that quiet acre of the dead on my way to the Wesley Oak. As I walked along the narrow path between the tombs, I suddenly saw on one of the graves the name, "Lucian Lamar Knight." It was my old classmate of Princeton days who had competed with me for the Paterson pulpit. He had written his own epitaph, in which he made no mention of his having been an ordained minister, but stating that he had been for forty years a ruling elder in the Presbyterian Church; and how he desired to "sleep the last, long sleep of eternity under the Wesley Oak, and by the waters of the Murmuring Altamaha." The epitaph ended with these words: "Here lies one who loved Georgia; every page of her history, every foot of her soil."

Soon after my visit to Paterson, I received a call to the First Presbyterian Church of that city. About the same time came a call from the church at Prairie du Sac. Never did a minister have two calls to more different churches: quiet, little Prairie du Sac on the darkly flowing Wisconsin River, and big, turbulent, smoking, half-foreign Paterson, on the Passaic River. The heart, of course, drew me to Prairie du Sac; but the call from Paterson had also a strong, though different, appeal. In what was called the "Prophet's Chamber" in Alexander Hall, because visiting speakers were entertained there, I consulted our lecturer in Homiletics, Dr. Burrell. After hearing an account of the two calls and the two congregations, Dr. Burrell said, "Go to Paterson." That settled it. To Paterson I went. Thus began my life's work. The Making of a Minister was finished. Not, of course, that the minister was finished, for, in a certain sense, my preparation for the work of the ministry was just beginning. But in another sense, and so far as background, home training and formal education were concerned, the training period was at an end. Now, as Paul put it, I was "put into the ministry." And, after all these years, I am still "in the ministry."

CHAPTER XIV

PATERSON

IN 1905, Paterson, New Jersey, was a city of one hundred twenty thousand inhabitants. It had been founded by the Society for Establishing Useful Manufactures, under the leadership of Alexander Hamilton. The falls of the Passaic River afforded abundant water power for the factories. The first inhabitants were of Dutch and English descent, the English having come from Nottingham to work in the silk mills. After the silk mills came the jute mills, the dye shops, and the locomotive works. Paterson at that time had an unenviable reputation, wholly undeserved. Whenever I told anyone I was going to Paterson, or that I lived in Paterson, the common reply was, "Oh, that's where the anarchists live!" This was due to the fact that Bresci, the anarchist who assassinated Humbert of Italy, had been a silk mill worker in Paterson, and at a meeting of anarchists who planned the assassination the lot fell on him. It might just as well have fallen on someone in Boston, Pittsburgh or Denver. There was also at that time the memory of a recent and most revolting crime. A beautiful young silk worker had been taken out by a number of men belonging to prominent families, repeatedly assaulted, and then left dead at her door. The trial was one of the most sensational in the history of the state, and received extraordinary publicity in the press of the whole country.

The city had a noble situation above and around the falls of the Passaic, but the river had been polluted by refuse and sewage poured into it from mills and factories in the towns above. In the Passaic River, a short distance above the falls, John P. Holland, inventor of the submarine, made one of his first under-water descents. I went frequently to the falls, whence I could look down on the city, and my church and parish. When I did so, I thought of the words of Andrew Bonar when he used to look down on his swarming parish in the Canongate in Edinburgh:

> *Sin worketh,*
> *Let me work too.*
> *Sin undoeth,*
> *Let me do.*
> *Busy as sin*
> *My work I'll ply,*
> *Till I rest in the rest*
> *Of Eternity.*

I was not unmindful, either, of what Samuel Rutherford, that great Covenanter lover of the Redeemer, used to say of his parish at Anworth on the Solway in Scotland:

> *Oh, Anworth by the Solway,*
> *To me thou still art dear.*
> *E'en from the port of heaven*
> *I'll drop for thee a tear.*
> *O, if one soul from Anworth*
> *Meet me at God's right hand,*
> *My heaven will be two heavens*
> *In Immanuel's Land.*

One of the first ministers to supply the church at Paterson, Hooper Cummings, stopped on a Sabbath afternoon on his way back to Newark to view the falls. In some way his young bride of a few weeks lost her footing and fell into the abyss and was drowned. Henceforth, there rested on the minister the shadow of a suspicion that he had pushed his wife over the falls. The suspicion was as unwarranted as that concerning the great preacher, T. DeWitt Talmage, when he was in Philadelphia, that when his boat was upset above the falls of the Schuylkill River he let his wife drown, but saved her sister, whom he afterwards married.

The history of the First Church of Paterson went back to 1794, when Sarah Colt gathered together a few children of the mill workers in her father's mansion on Ward Street and taught them the truths of the Bible. Thus the Sunday School of the First Church is one of the oldest, if not the oldest, in America. The Colt family afterwards established the Colt Arms Factory at New Haven, Connecticut.

The church edifice was a large brick building, in appearance not unlike the Cathedral of St. Francis at Assisi in Italy. The church property covered a triangular block in the very heart of Paterson. Every one of the three churches I have had the privilege to serve, the First Church of Paterson, the Arch Street Church in Philadelphia, and the First Church of Pittsburgh, have been so located. I have thanked God for that. In all my churches I could hear, as it were, the pulse beat of the city and the deep diapason note of its sins and sorrows.

Adjoining the church was the chapel, and between church and chapel a lawn, with gracious elm trees shading it. Just across the street from the chapel was the brownstone Passaic Count Jail. Sometimes those who wanted to go to the church went to the jail by mistake, and vice versa. One day I received word that a young man in the jail desired to see me. I went across and found a young man, about my own age, an insurance agent, who had kept back some of the payments he had collected, but with the purpose of refunding as soon as he could. For this offense he was arrested and committed to the jail. The insurance company told him that if the shortage were made good they would not press the charges against him. I thought it was too bad that a young man should have the stigma of a jail sentence on him, and paid the sum he owed the company. I also gave him sufficient money to get to his home in central New York. He was profuse in his thanks, wrung my hand, and assured me that I would soon hear from him and get back the money I had paid on his behalf.

That was in 1905. In 1925, twenty years afterwards, I was in Columbus, Ohio, to preach the sermon at the opening of the General Assembly of the Presbyterian Church, in my capacity as Moderator. As I was standing in the crowd in the lobby of the hotel the night before the Assembly opened, a man accosted me and asked if I remembered him. I responded with the usual courteous evasion, that there was something familiar about him, but that I could not remember his name. He then asked me if I recalled getting a young man out of the Passaic County Jail twenty years before. He was the young man, now a middle-aged shoe merchant in a central New York city. He said he had followed my career and had often thought of me, and had purposed to get in touch with me. I was wondering why he had not done so, when he drew out his wallet and took therefrom a number of bills and handed them to me, saying as he did so, "Here is the money you gave me, with interest for all these years." When I put the money in my pocket, I thought of the verse in the Book of Ecclesiastes, "Cast thy bread upon the waters: for thou shalt find it after many days."

I wish now I had kept a record of all those whom,

through the years, I have helped, out of my own funds or those of the church. The most difficult ones to refuse, of course, were the women, with their tears and pathetic tales. In Philadelphia most of those who came for assistance wanted me to help them to get to New York, and I used to say that if I had helped as many people to Heaven as I had to New York, my ministry would not be without fruit.

The ruse of one clever rogue comes back to me now. He appeared one day at my study in Philadelphia, saying he was the son of a Presbyterian minister in the West. It was just after World War I, and he was still in uniform. He said his brother was at the Y.M.C.A., and could not attend the services at the church because he had been shell-shocked, and was likely to make an outcry in the midst of the service. He told me he had secured a job in the men's clothing department of the John Wanamaker store, but that he could not begin his work until he had a suit of civilian clothes. To make sure, I called the head of the men's department at Wanamakers, who told me that the young man had been given a job, but that he must have civilian clothes before he could start work. Thus assured, I gave him the money for a suit, and he was to report at the end of the week when he received his first payment. Not hearing from him, I called the store and learned that he had never showed up at all. He had worked the same skillful deception on two other ministers of the city.

The first man who got money from me, and never returned it, was a Congregational minister who called on me shortly after I went to Paterson, and outlined an ambitious, and quite sensible, scheme of ministerial insurance and pension. At the end he asked me for fifty dollars, which I was foolish and soft-hearted enough to give him. But when I think of that one man whom I saved from a prison sentence, and who twenty years afterwards returned what I had given him, and with interest, I feel that it was worth while being deceived by many, if per chance I could help an honest few. I could never be quite so firm and severe as another minister to whom I referred a man who came to see me and asked for help in those early days at Paterson. He told me he was recently released from Sing Sing after serving a sentence for forgery. To illustrate his skill in that line, he took a piece of paper and signed a name and wrote a sentence in half a dozen different hands, an old man's, a businessman's, a woman's and a child's, and so on. I always felt anxious afterwards because he had me write out my own signature and then showed me how closely he could imitate it. But no forged check ever came back to me.

After this lesson in forgery, the man told me that whatever cities he went to his record was known, and the police ordered him to move on. He despaired of getting a job and starting a life over again in an honest way, and, therefore, had decided to put an end to his life. His purpose in coming to me, he said, was to have me write a farewell letter to his mother. Moved by this tale, I talked with him and prayed with him, and in the end seemed to persuade him that life was still worth living. He said he came from Albany, New York, and had had some association with the Presbyterian church of that city. I gave him some money and clothing, and, to make sure, bought him a ticket for Albany and saw him off on the train at the Paterson station. About the same time I had occasion to go to Albany and, when changing trains in the station there, I called up the Presbyterian minister and asked him about this man whom I had helped. The man, by the way, had said that he was going to end his life by jumping into the Passaic River. The minister who knew him of old, at once ejaculated, "That's what you ought to have told him to do! That would have been the best thing he ever did in his life!"

Some very carefully deliberated and helpful sayings of a preacher will be forgotten, whereas some light and playful remark will long be remembered. On the tenth anniversary of my ordination I preached a sermon, "Ten Years in the Ministry," in the course of which I happened to say a word about the kind of appeals a minister receives, and the many imposters who come to him for help, and remarked, "When I get word in my study that a strange man wants to see me, I lay aside my wallet and go down; but if it is a woman, I put on the whole armor of God and go down." Twenty-five years afterwards, when I was addressing a gathering of ministers at the Montreat Assembly, North Carolina, and had finished my lecture on "Preaching Without Notes," I threw the meeting open for questions. One of the first questions asked was this, "Is it true that you once said that when a strange man was announced you laid aside your wallet and went down, but that if it was a woman, you 'put on the whole armor of God and went down'?" I had forgotten the incident and the saying until it was recalled to me. I told them it was true, and not altogether nonsense, either.

On my first arrival at Paterson on a January night in 1905, I took a horse cab at the Erie station. The manse where I was to be entertained was not more than two or three blocks distant, but the shrewd cabbie, in order to get a good fare, took me quite a ride around the town before he deposited me at the door of the manse, where I was greeted by the widow of the late pastor of the church, Dr. Franklin E. Miller. Dr. Miller was a man of superior character and intelligence, and had commanded a Negro regiment in the Civil War, a thing which it took high courage to do, because of the attitude of Confederate soldiers towards Negro troops and their officers.

Some time before Dr. Miller came to the First Church from the First Presbyterian Church of Easton, Pennsylvania, there had been a peaceful secession from the church. A group of the congregation had organized a new church and had put up a handsome edifice in what was then the residential part of the city. Most of the families of wealth left the First Church and united with this new Church of the Redeemer, which called the then pastor of the First Church, Dr. David Magie. Dr. Miller, apparently, had not fully understood the situation in the Paterson Church, and was disappointed from the start. He had a military way with him and got into frequent difficulties, which resulted in another secession. At the time I was called to the church there had been considerable discussion about selling the very valuable property and removing to the residential part of the city; but as the congregation began to pick up, this was dropped and forgotten.

On that first Sabbath morning, with snow piled waist-high along the sidewalk, I walked up Ward Street, past the post office and the Passaic County Court House, to the church, which stood on the corner of Main and Ward. In the vestibule a slight, kindly man met me with a smile, saying, "Is this our minister for today?" He was Albert Jones, always spoken of as "Jones, the Hatter," for that was the day of special stores in the retail business. The church had a massive bell in its tower which used to shake the building when it was rung. At one time it was connected with the fire department of the city and rang out the fire alarm. When the trustees were considering the request of the city for such use of the bell, some objected on the ground that the ringing of the bell on the Sabbath would disturb the worship of the congregation. Socrates Tuttle, father of Mrs. Hobart, widow of Vice President Garret A. Hobart, a keen lawyer, and noted for his wit, answered the objection, saying, "Dr. Hornblower has been giving us a fire alarm every Sunday for the last twenty-five years, and nobody in the congregation has ever been disturbed!" Dr. William H. Hornblower was for many years the distinguished pastor of the First Church, and afterwards a professor at the Western Theological Seminary. He was the father of the eminent New York lawyer, William Hornblower, nominated by President Cleveland as an Associate Justice of the United States Supreme Court, but not confirmed by the Senate.

On the wall of the church was a large black slate tablet to the memory of the Rev. Mr. and Mrs. Robert McMullen, missionaries to India, who perished at Cawnpore in the Sepoy Mutiny. Just back of the church lay a shabby section, but once the homes of the chief citizens, known as "Dublin." When I came, many of the Irish had given way to the Italians, who had a church just back of the First Church and staged great processions, just as in Italy, on special days, carrying aloft an image of the Virgin. In a miserable tenement in "Dublin" I encountered one of the most shocking cases of parental cruelty and of the degradation caused by drink, that I have ever known. The little girl was in my Sunday School, and I went to call at her home. It was just after Christmas. The expectant child had hung up her stocking, and early on Christmas morning had eagerly arisen and run to see what was in her stocking, only to find it filled with stones! "What man is there of you, whom if his son ask bread, will give him a stone?" Christ asked, intimating that to do so would be the worst kind of inhumanity. But here was a father who did.

In that same "Dublin" section, too, I attended the first deathbed and saw for the first time the passing of a soul. She was a fine young woman, a singer in the choir. When I first went into the room, standing a little apart, and somewhat timid, I started to pray; but the mother, who was sitting at the bedside, interrupted me, saying, "Come a little closer, Mr. Macartney." I have never forgotten that, and it taught

144

me at the very beginning to try to come close to the sorrows and burdens of my people. While I was in the room the young woman breathed her last. The mother's brother, a mail carrier, had just come into the room, and when he saw what had happened, he folded his weeping sister in his arms in a tender and comforting embrace which I can still see. The public thinks of the minister chiefly in the pulpit; but often it will not be in the pulpit, but in the sick chamber and by the side of the dying that he will do his chief ministry, where, far removed from the excitement and glare of publicity, he wins his chief trophies. Would that all of us when we start our ministry, and when we draw near to its close, as some of us are doing, could bear in mind the text of the first sermon of Jesus that day in the synagogue of Nazareth, "The Spirit of the Lord is upon me, because he hath anointed me to preach the gospel to the poor; he hath sent me to heal the brokenhearted."

I had been licensed by the Presbytery of Philadelphia, after passing a real examination, in which we submitted a Latin thesis. Mine was on the Advents of Christ, "De Adventibus Christi." Dr. Matthew Hyndmann, who examined us in the languages, continued to do that for almost fifty years for the Presbytery of Philadelphia. The Presbytery of Jersey City ordained me on an October night in 1905 at the First Church in Paterson. Dr. John DeWitt of Princeton Seminary preached the sermon, Dr. Charles Shaw of the Second Church charged the congregation, and Dr. David J. Burrell, pastor of the Marble Collegiate Church, New York, charged the minister; and my honored father made the ordaining prayer, as he had done for all his other sons in the ministry, save Robertson, whose town, Oconto, Wisconsin, was too remote for Father to go to. In his ordaining prayer, as he lay his hands on my head, Father spoke of how I had been called to "this fruitful vineyard." I trust that, in some degree at least, the eight and one-half years I spent in Paterson fulfilled Father's prediction.

In charging me, Dr. Burrell told the congregation a story which has been long remembered. One cold dark night in Glasgow, Scotland, a minister was summoned to the bedside of a dying woman. He made his way through the wet streets, down the "close," and up the stairs to a lofty and wretched chamber, where he found a poor woman on her bed, sick with a contagious disease. After repeating some appropriate verses of Scripture to her, and after a prayer, he rose to go. As he was leaving, he said to the woman, "I don't seem to recognize you as a member of my parish." "No," said the woman, "I belong to Dr. McCleod's parish." Somewhat put out that this woman, ill with a contagious disease, had summoned him instead of her own minister, the famous Norman McCleod, he said to her, "Why in the world did not you call your own minister?" "Hoot, mon," the woman replied, "we couldna spare Normie!"

In one section of Paterson there was a vile theater, "for men only." Through a man on the staff of the chief Paterson newspaper, I learned the facts about the scenes which transpired at this theater, and on a Sunday night let go with both barrels. The manager of the theater threatened to sue me, but as the reporter of the newspaper was ready to confirm what I had said, nothing came of the suit. A short time afterwards, when I was at dinner one night with the two doctors with whom I lived in Paterson, Dr. David and Dr. Edna Carlough, the maid announced two callers at the door. I went out to the front living-room where I saw two rather flashily dressed young women. There was something about them which at once aroused my suspicion and put me on my guard. I asked them to be seated, and, excusing myself for a moment, went back to the dining room, and then returned, leaving both doors behind me open. One of the women then made some inquiry about the baptism of a child. I stated the conditions upon which a minister of the Presbyterian Church is permitted to baptize a child, namely, that one of the parents must be a professed Christian and a member of the church. Then the woman shifted her ground and asked me if I would bless the ring with which she had been married a short time before. I told her that it was not the custom of most Protestant ministers to bless a marriage ring, and especially so long after the marriage. There was an awkward silence for a time, as if they were thinking up some other question to ask, and then they arose and left. Perhaps I was mistaken, but I have always felt that they had been sent, perhaps by those who had been angered at my attack on the vile theater, to put me in a compromising position, one of them falling on the floor or screaming; but seeing that the doors were open into the dining room, desisted from their evil purpose. Long years afterward, a friend in Paterson told me that the editor of a yellow sheet had, about that time, sent a woman to call upon me with the purpose of injuring my reputation. She came with the pretext of asking some questions in religious matters which troubled her; but said afterwards that she was treated so courteously, and given such frank and earnest answers, that she felt ashamed of herself for what she had come to do and refused to carry out her evil part. All of this will remind the minister that what Christ said to his disciples still holds, "Be ye wise as serpents and harmless as doves."

A block down Main Street from the First Church was St. John's Roman Catholic Cathedral. The rector, Dean William McNulty, was a familiar and much loved personality in Paterson. He wore a cape over his shoulders, a fur cap, a fringe of white whiskers about his face, and went about with his right arm thrust under his cape and his head bent a little to one side. A very life-like statue in front of St. John's

Cathedral shows him in that posture. He was active in a Catholic Total Abstinence Society, and on a Saturday night would frequently go into the saloons and haul out from them some of his parishioners.

Near the Cathedral was the Third Presbyterian Church, presided over by a rough and original Irishman, Dr. Joshua B. Gallaway. At a meeting of the General Assembly, when the adoption of the Book of Common Worship was before the Assembly, Dr. Gallaway strongly opposed such adoption, and, to illustrate the folly of "canned" prayers, related the following anecdote. Two men were passing through a field in the country when they were charged by a bull. They started for the nearest fence; but it was soon apparent that they could not make it before the bull would be upon them. One said to the other, "Put up a prayer, John, we're in for it!" But John answered, "I can't, I never made a public prayer in my life." "But you must," said his companion, "the bull will soon be on us. Pray, John, and pray quickly!" "All right," said John, "I'll give you the only prayer I know, the one my father used to repeat at the table, O, Lord, for what we are about to receive, make us truly thankful!"

The minister of the Second Church was an accomplished and talented old gentleman, Dr. Charles D. Shaw. He was a very large man, wore a long Prince Albert and a stovepipe hat which added much to his stature as he walked down Broadway with a very short wife on his arm. He had been at the Second Church before, and then at the First Church at Springfield, Illinois, where Lincoln had had a pew, and then, not liking the free and easy ways of the West, had returned to Paterson. His study desk was a mountain of tumbled and disordered papers; but that disorder on his desk was never reflected in his preaching. I went once to call on him when he was ill. I was surprised to see him sitting up and dressed, and said, quoting part of a New Testament verse, but not thinking about the rest of the verse, "Well, doctor, I'm glad to see you sitting up and clothed——." Then I did remember the rest of the sentence and stopped; whereupon Dr. Shaw quickly finished that verse about the possessed Gadarene, "If not in my right mind."

I have in my library a commentary given me by a retired Lutheran minister whom I would frequently meet on Grand Street, going to or from a beer saloon, with a bucket in his hand. That used to be spoken of as "rushing the growler." Dr. Hamilton was the popular Rector of St. Paul's Church on Broadway. I remember once passing the churchhouse where they used to have entertainments and dances, and this night some of the young people continued to dance on the street in front of the church. About that time the First Church had completed a building for Sabbath School, institutional and social work. It was called Memorial Hall, in honor of Alfred W. Barnes, a well-known Paterson chemical manufacturer, an elder and a trustee in the church, a faithful friend of the minister, and a most generous friend of the church. Dr. Hamilton met me on the street one day and asked me what activities we proposed to have in the new building. When I told him, he said, with the greatest emphasis, "Never let in dancing! If you let that camel's head in, it will take possession of the whole tent." I have never let it in any of the churches I have served, for it is death to spiritual life in a congregation.

Most of the churches of that day, and a great many today, are dark and forbidding at their portals. One of the first things I did at Paterson was to install bright lights about the entrance of the church, and an electric sign. I did the same at Philadelphia and Pittsburgh. Let there be Light! That first winter in Paterson I preached a series of evening sermons on some of the Bible characters, mostly Old Testament characters. I advertised these sermons with window

149

cards. The response was immediate, and I learned at the very beginning of my ministry that biographical preaching strikes a popular chord. I preached also series on the great doctrines; and, on occasions, took for a subject, but always with Biblical background, some great contemporary event in the world.

I was not unmindful in my preaching of the temperance reform which, with great excitement, was then sweeping the land in the form of "local option." I was sounded out about becoming a field representative of the Anti-Saloon League. I had no thought of taking such a post, but in a letter to my father I mentioned the matter to him. In his reply he gave me good advice, "Stick to your last." With a great company of ministers and others, I went down to Trenton to attend the hearing before the Legislature on the Local Option Bill. The liquor interests had secured the services of a distinguished lawyer, a former attorney general of the United States. Long years before, he had been a Sabbath School teacher in the First Church. I happened one summer day to be worshiping in the Presbyterian Church at Bedford, Pennsylvania. After the service I fell into conversation with one of the elders, and when he learned that I was from Paterson, he asked about this lawyer who had been his classmate at Lafayette College, saying that among all of the students he was the outstanding, enthusiastic Christian leader. I had then to tell him how his brilliant friend's light had been quenched. Ichabod! The glory hath departed!

In that hearing before the New Jersey Legislature the liquor interests put up also an Episcopal minister to speak against local option and prohibition. His speech, coming from a clergyman, was so offensive that he was frequently interrupted by the opposition. Once I myself cried out, "Judas Iscariot!" Whereupon a big saloon-keeper next to me pushed me in the ribs, saying, "Keep still! Your side

had its chance. Now listen to our side." But that ejacula-
tion on my part, "Judas Iscariot," was, I felt, a good witness
and one of the best sermons I ever preached. Sometimes
our most effective sermons will be preached in that way. One
afternoon at Canton, Ohio, where I was to preach at a Lenten
service, I took a taxicab at the station and drove to the hotel.
It was wartime, and the driver asked permission to stop at
a home on the way, where he picked up three others, a man,
a woman, and a young boy. The man was about thirty-five,
red-faced, and evidently some kind of a well-paid artisan. He
began to talk with the woman about some of their friends or
relatives, using the most shocking profanity. My conscience
prodded me. Ought I not remonstrate with him? But that
is always hard to do, and this fellow was a man of most violent
spirit. But when I got out at the hotel, and was paying my
fare, I mustered up courage to say to the man, looking at
the boy at his side, "How old is this boy?" When he told me,
I said, "Don't you think he ought to hear a little better language?" Immediately, and in a great rage, the man de-
nounced me, saying, with great oaths, that that was none of
my —— business. I made no rejoinder, and the cab drove on.
In a way, I thought that I had failed, and yet, the woman,
the boy and the man himself will probably never forget the
incident. That night at least, preaching on the Atonement
to a great congregation, I had unusual "liberty of utterance"
because of the far more difficult sermon I had preached to
the profane swearer in the cab that afternoon.

Between the church and the Sunday School building at
Paterson, there was a spacious lawn, shaded by several beautiful elm trees. Crowds of people were always passing along
Main Street in front of the church, and I resolved to try the
experiment of a Sunday night service on the lawn. It went
well from the first. We had good music and good lighting.
Chairs were set out on the lawn and were always filled; but

the far larger congregation stood on the sidewalk beyond the iron fence. Perhaps in the Great Day, when all secrets shall be revealed, I shall learn that some of the seed sown on those Sunday nights fell on good ground, and sprang up and bore fruit unto eternal life. It is a great thing for the preacher if he can always hold to that hope as he preaches, and have the confidence that God's Word "shall not return unto him void."

One of the delights of my ministry has been preaching to large groups of men, such as the Tuesday Noon Club at Pittsburgh. I served my apprenticeship at that kind of preaching at Paterson. Some Christian men, conductors and motormen on the street railway, wanted a service for the employees. One day every week I used to go down to the car barns at noon and speak to the large assembly of men. I formed among them some warm friendships and always tried to give them a helpful gospel message. These meetings also gave me an opportunity to come into close touch with the working man.

The First Church had two mission churches, one at Albion Place on Garrett Mountain, the other in Totowa. This latter, in time, became an independent church. With a generous initial gift from my friend Mrs. Hobart, I managed to raise sufficient funds to erect a church. In the midst of these activities I tried to be faithful in pastoral visitation, calling once every year in all the homes of the congregation. In one home at the close of the visit I said to the woman, "Shall we have prayer together?" With a startled look on her face, she answered, "Do you think I need it?" As I remember, I replied, "Well, I think we all need it." I think now of just three times when I asked if I might have prayer with people and received a negative answer. One was this time at Paterson, and the other two in Pittsburgh; once in a hospital when a wife declined my proposal to pray for her sick husband, and again in a luxurious home in a stylish apartment-hotel, where I had been summoned by a sick wife. The husband, a high industrialist, had become sour on religion and the church, and received me very coldly. When I asked him if he would go in with me to his wife's bedroom while I prayed with her, he bluntly refused. Of all the people who deserve our pity and prayers, it is a woman who has deep spiritual yearning and a love for Christ and the Church, but has a husband who resents her Christian interest and faith.

Paterson was frequently torn by industrial strife, and the silk mills were often shut down because of strikes. Those were the days of the I.W.W., the Industrial Workers of the World. On an open lot I heard Bill Haywood, the radical labor leader of that day, address a gathering of strikers. Emma Goldman was also there. Haywood had achieved notoriety in his trial for murder after a dynamiting in Idaho. He was acquitted, but the young prosecutor secured national fame through his handling of the case for the Commonwealth. He was the future Senator from Idaho, William E. Borah. Haywood was a powerful speaker, and so was Emma Goldman. After World War I, they were both expelled to Russia. Some time before her death, Miss Goldman wrote a book which reveals her complete disillusionment with the Russian revolution and way of life. It would be a good cure for our so-called Reds, and all others who say the United States is no better than Russia, if, like Haywood and Goldman, they were sent to Russia to live for a season.

I was not often off duty from my own pulpit, but once or twice I heard the celebrated Dr. Charles H. Parkhurst at the noonday service in his marble temple at Madison Square. One would never have thought of him then as the preacher who had stirred and shaken New York, for the fire then burned very low. On a Sunday afternoon I heard Dr. William Rogers Richards at the Brick Presbyterian Church on the text from Ecclesiastes, "He that observeth the wind shall not sow." It was a carefully prepared and closely read sermon, in the course of which he remarked that although ministers had to go out in all kinds of weather, rain or shine, hot or cold, snow or hail, and had to go to the cemetery on the most inclement days, they were always rated as a good risk by the insurance companies.

The automobile hearse and funeral car did not appear in Paterson until some time after I began my ministry there, and many was the long cold ride I had, especially to some far distant cemetery, in the horse-drawn carriages, with my feet in straw or on a hot brick. But the old-time funeral was a much more impressive and stately affair than the present ones with the white-flag-marked automobiles rushing through the streets. Then the undertaker, crowned with his high silk hat, sat aloft in state on the top of the plumed hearse. The funeral processions always seemed to pass down the main street of the city. Once when the funeral was at a house in "Dublin," just near the road which led to the cemetery in Totowa, the undertaker, Mr. McDonald, a splendid figure of a man, both on the street and on top of the hearse, took us back to the main street and then out to the cemetery, a very roundabout journey. When I protested against these long detours, he said that if he were to omit the parade down Main Street the family would be sure to reproach him and would feel that they were not getting their money's worth. Sometimes you will hear persons refer to an undertaker as the symbol of lugubriousness and gloom. Oliver Wendell Holmes said that he was turned aside from entering the ministry because of a clergyman who looked and talked like an undertaker. Yet, as a matter of fact and experience, I have found the undertakers to be extraordinarily good company, and many are the pleasant and profitable conversations I have had with them on our rides together.

When I began my ministry, all the funerals were held

in homes. Now they are nearly all held in a funeral home.
The last word in funeral homes was, and still is, the establishment of Oliver Bair on Chestnut Street, Philadelphia.
Once on a long funeral ride together, Oliver Bair told me the
history of his life as an undertaker, and what a great venture
it was, especially in Philadelphia, America's most conservative city, to establish a funeral home. How often I conducted
services in that remarkable place: beautiful paintings, costly
rugs, richly carved chairs, and the air of refinement such as
one meets in a private home of wealth and distinction.
There were guest rooms, bedrooms, and dining rooms for
those who came with their dead from out of the city. The
funeral rooms, or halls, were numerous, and as one conducted
a service, one could sometimes hear in the distance the voice
of another minister as he intoned the service for the dead.
And yet, whether it is a bare shabby room in Paterson's
"Dublin," or Oliver Bair's stately funeral home on Chestnut
Street, or the mansion of the wealthy, death is always the
same. People sometimes ask me if that is not a terrible and
oppressive thing in a minister's life, having to go to so many
funerals. My answer is always, No. The explanation is, that
in trying to comfort and help other souls, and as the representative of Christ, the minister speaks the only words of
hope that can be spoken over the dead. In addition to this,
death has an eloquence and impressiveness all its own. As
Sir Walter Raleigh so nobly phrased it, "O, eloquent, just
and mighty Death! whom none could advise, thou hast persuaded; what none hath dared, thou hast done; and whom
all the world hath flattered, thou only hast cast out of the
world and despised. Thou hast drawn together all the far
stretched greatness, all the pride, cruelty and ambition of
man, and covered it all over with these two narrow words,
Hic jacet!" These are the reasons why I never felt that the
many hours I have spent at funerals were wasted time, and

why I begin to understand what the Preacher of Ecclesiastes meant when he said, "It is better to go to the house of mourning than to the house of feasting: for that is the end of all men, and the living will lay it to his heart." I have often been bored at the house of feasting and merrymaking, but never at the house of mourning.

In 1909 I took my second trip abroad. I sailed on the then queen of the seas, the Cunard liner *Lusitania*. I landed at Liverpool, visited Chester with its arcaded streets and its venerable cathedral, then went down to Stratford on Avon, and then on to London, where I had a look at the House of Commons in session, the members of this supposed Gibraltar of democracy and free government lolling about, hats on, feet on the table, almost under the Speaker's nose. From London I went down to Winchester and saw its noble cathedral, the most beautifully set of all the cathedrals; then on to Salisbury, with its incomparable spire, and out to the Stonehenge, the impressive ruins of the worship of the Druids; and so on to Southampton, where I took a boat for St. Helier on the Island of Jersey. On the Sabbath evening I walked along the steep cliffs and looked across the water towards Guernsey, another Channel island, and thought of Victor Hugo's great tale which had Guernsey for its background, that tremendous lesson in conscience and retribution, "The Toilers of the Sea." Then I went across to France and up to Paris, and from Paris to Geneva. At Alesia, near the Swiss border, I thought of the thesis I had written at the University of Wisconsin on Caesar's siege of Alesia.

At Geneva I had a somewhat unusual, and also amusing, experience. One evening, walking on the promenade of the new town, I met a Paterson banker and a neighboring Presbyterian minister. The minister and I arranged to meet the next morning and visit the places of interest in Old Geneva, the University, St. Peter's Church where John Cal-

vin preached, John Knox's Chapel, and Calvin's house. I
was staying at a hotel far out in the Old Town. When I
awoke the next morning, it was with the feeling that I had
overslept. When I looked at my watch it said eleven o'clock.
That confirmed my feeling that I had overslept. "Too fast
travelling," I said to myself; "spending the nights on the train
and sightseeing by day." When I came downstairs I said
something to the concierge about having overslept this time
for sure; but he did not seem to take in what I had said. I
had no thought of getting breakfast in the hotel at that late
hour, and went out on the street to search for a restaurant.
But wherever I went the chairs of the street restaurants
were set up on the tables. Breakfast must be over, I thought,
and now they are clearing the decks for the next meal. Break-
fastless, I made my way to Thomas Cook & Company to cash
a traveller's check, but found an iron curtain down over the
doors of their office. Then I recalled that it was Saturday,
and that the places of business must be closed on Saturday
afternoon. The whole town seemed strangely quiet and deserted. But I had an explanation for that too. They were
having an all-Swiss Band Tournament that week in one of
the city parks, and I concluded that the reason for the empty
streets must be that most of the inhabitants had gone out
to the band tournament.

I felt sure that it was too late now to find my friend;
nevertheless I crossed the lake by Rousseau's Island and
made my way to the Beau Rivage, where I handed my card
to the concierge and asked him to take it up to my friend if
he were still in the hotel. For some reason he seemed to be
reluctant to comply with my request, but at length, after
much urging, he disappeared with my card. Presently he
came down, saying that my friend would see me in his room.
When I went up I found him in bed. I thought nothing of
that, for I knew that he was not an early riser. He rubbed

his eyes, and we talked together for a little about Geneva. At length I said to him, referring to our plans to visit the places of interest, "If we are going to do anything today, we had better get started, for it is now half-past twelve." He looked at me in astonishment, exclaiming, "What's the matter with you?" Then he put his hand under his pillow and pulled out his watch—it was just 7:30 in the morning! It was a case in which everything, up to the very end, fitted into the delusion with which I had awakened, that I had long overslept. It was a case, too, which shows how we cannot always be certain on the ground of circumstantial evidence.

From Geneva, I made my way to Basel; thence into Germany to Heidelberg, and then down the Rhine to Cologne with its magnificent Gothic cathedral. When I was buying my ticket at Basel, a fellow citizen, and not the most desirable type, who had heard me tell the ticket agent where and how I wanted to go, said to him, "Give me a ticket just like you sold this man." The fellow stuck to me like a burr on a good part of my trip through Germany.

When I boarded the train at Cologne, there was no room in the compartment where I got a seat for my bag, and I left it, with my hat and overcoat, in the aisle, and went into the diner. When I came back, bag, coat and hat were gone. When we crossed the frontier into Holland, the Dutch customs officers, not finding anyone who claimed the baggage, had taken it off at the border town. A rather pompous young American who claimed to have high connections at Washington, made a great noise to the conductor about the lost baggage. But whether it was that, or my own quieter inquiry, the baggage arrived soon after I did at my Amsterdam hotel. The next day I set out with my new-found friend in a taxicab to see the sights of Amsterdam, the Canals, the Rycks Museum with its Rembrandt masterpieces, and the diamond shops and cutters. The taxicab had just made its appearance in London and on the continent, some time before it was seen on the streets of New York, and it was quite an event then to ride in one. But whenever we stopped, my companion ordered the taxi driver to wait on us. This he did, but always with the meter mounting higher and higher. I soon saw that my meager budget could not stand such a pace, and the next day gave my spend-thrift friend the slip and set out by myself for The Hague and Delftshaven, the sailing port of the Pilgrims.

The only time I felt uneasy about my surroundings was at Brussels. A runner for a hotel, a disreputable-looking fellow, got hold of my bag and conducted me to a rather shabby-looking hotel. For some reason I felt apprehensive lest I should be robbed. It certainly looked like a den of evil, and I took my bag and found another hotel. The next day I went out to Waterloo, where I climbed the mount with its famous lion on the top. I looked down on those rich fields which lay all about in the golden sunlight, where the poppies were growing and the harvesters were bending with the sickle and the scythe, and where in a few years would lie the dead and dying of World War I.

From Belgium I went back to England and crossed over to Ireland, stopping at Dublin. I had always been much interested in Dean Swift, and once gave a lecture on his life and writings. In the gloomy cathedral in Dublin, I read his strange and somewhat bitter epitaph "Ubi saeva indignatio utterius cor lacerare nequit," "Where burning indignation can no longer tear his heart." I rode horseback through the Gap of Dunloe, sailed over Killarney Lake, and kissed the Blarney Stone. My cash was now running very low. When in the morning the red-headed waiter in full dress brought me back my change on a silver tray, after I had paid my bill, and saw me meditating as I picked up the shillings, he said to me, reading my countenance and the concern in my mind,

"Does it hurt you, Sir? Does it hurt you, Sir? If it does, I'll be glad to make you a loan." He certainly was an unusual head waiter, but I quickly assured him that it did not hurt me at all. But that night in the hotel at Queenstown, now Cobh, where we were to board the *Lusitania* the next morning, I dined with an American professor and his wife who had held my feet, and I theirs, when we kissed the Blarney Stone. We had quite a debate at the end of the dinner over which of us should pay the bill. He finally won the debate, and fortunately for me, for I did not have the money to pay it. The *Lusitania* had been held up for a day, and there was another night's expense at the hotel. I was able to make the deck of the *Lusitania* the next afternoon with just a few shillings in my pocket. On the run westward to New York, the *Lusitania* broke the world record for speed, and there was great excitement and much betting among the passengers. Six years later, and just off Queenstown, the *Lusitania*, torpedoed by a German submarine, went down in one of the most tragic and terrible of marine disasters, carrying with her fifteen hundred persons. On my last visit to Queenstown, when waiting for the steamer, I went to the cemetery on top of the hill back of the town to visit the tomb of Charles Wolfe, the Irish poet, and the author of those almost perfect lines, "The Burial of Sir John Moore."

> *Not a drum was heard, not a funeral note*
> *As his corse to the rampart we hurried,*
> *Not a soldier discharged his farewell shot*
> *O'er the grave where our hero we buried. . . .*
> *We carved not a line, and we raised not a stone,*
> *But we left him alone with his glory.*

Wolfe was not only a great poet, but also a powerful and eloquent preacher. In one of his sermons he spoke on the

Judgment to Come. In the sermon he said, "The judgments of God fall often enough in this world to let us know that God judges; but seldom enough to let us know that there is a judgment hereafter."

In 1912, in company with my brother Albert, I made another trip to Europe, sailing on the Danish steamer, *C. F. Tietgen.* It was a long, fog-shrouded trip of almost two weeks, clear around the north of Scotland and the Orkney Islands, before we landed at Kristiansand in Norway. On shipboard I made the acquaintance of a very delightful and distinguished gentleman, our Ambassador to Denmark, Maurice Francis Egan. Dr. Egan was an author of note, and had written one of the best books on St. Francis of Assisi. He was a devout Roman Catholic. I was talking with him about the way in which he wrote his books, and he asked me about my method of writing my sermons. It was he who suggested to me the method which I have followed now for so many years, that of dictating directly to the typewriter. While at sea we got a wireless saying that Woodrow Wilson had been nominated for the Presidency at the Democratic Convention at Baltimore. A number of us who had been at Princeton, and others who rejoiced in the tidings, staged a parade and celebration on the deck. When at Paterson I heard Wilson speak twice; once in the opera house when he was a candidate for the governorship of New Jersey, and once when he was Governor and was a candidate for the Presidential nomination. It looked strange to see him on the platform with the leaders of the Democratic party in Passaic County, the most prominent of them well-known brewers and distillers. It would remind one of what was said of Clay's association with John Quincy Adams, who made some kind of a deal which resulted in Adams' election to the Presidency when the election was thrown into the House of Representatives, "The Puritan and the Blackleg."

An important part of my training at Paterson was in the many addresses I was invited to make in the city and in nearby towns. The Grand Army of the Republic learned of my interest in the Civil War, and I frequently spoke at their gatherings. The then principal of the only high school in Paterson was Dr. Jacob A. Reinhart. He frequently worshiped at the First Church, and often asked me to speak at the high school. As the years went by, I had accumulated a mass of information about the battles of the Civil War, and had taken many photographs of the battlefields. With these pictures I gave on many occasions my illustrated lecture, "Highways and Byways of the Civil War." At that time the New York City Board of Education had a series of popular lectures, which were given at night in the public schools and were open to the public. I went into New York one day to interview Dr. Henry M. Leipzger, who had charge of these lectures. He was a rather brusque, gruff man, and not once during the interview did he lift up his head from his desk to look at me. But after I had described the lecture, he said he would put me on his list, and set a date for the first lecture. I gave a number of these lectures on the Civil War in New York and in Brooklyn, and was astonished at the crowds which came to hear them, especially the foreign groups, which one would not think would be much interested in our Civil War.

The minister ought to give careful thought to his vacation period, lest the time be spent without profit. Many of my own vacations were spent following in the footsteps of the Apostle Paul, and many others traversing the battlefields of the Civil War.

However, one of the most pleasant and memorable of my vacations was a short trip taken through Canada in company with the Rev. Alford Boggs, the then pastor of the Princeton Presbyterian Church, Philadelphia. He joined

me at Paterson, and we set out together on the Erie railroad
for Niagara Falls, and then on to Toronto. We lived in state
at the King Edward Hotel, but cut down expenses by getting
our meals at a dairy lunch. Leaving Toronto, we travelled
westward to Galt, where I was to preach on the Sabbath in
the United Presbyterian Church. In the evening Mr. Boggs
went over to the Presbyterian Church, then the largest Presbyterian congregation in Canada, where he heard the Rev.
Robert Edward Knowles, and a popular author of the day,
preach. I joined him at Mr. Knowles' manse after the service.
We spent a pleasant hour at the manse, and then started for
the humble cottage where we were being entertained. We
had been running short of funds, and were counting much
on the honorarium which I was to receive for my services at
the United Presbyterian Church. On the way to our cottage
we stopped under a street lamp to open the envelope. It
contained just fifteen dollars!

During the night Mr. Boggs awakened with the fearful
dread that he was going blind. I too was disturbed at his distress, and got up and worked up and down the slats of the
venetian blind on the window, until at length it became evident that my friend was still able to see. We took the train
in the morning back to Toronto. Neither one of us had at
that time that somewhat useless appendage to our names,
the honorary degree of Doctor of Divinity. Nevertheless, to
amuse ourselves, we had fallen into the habit of addressing
one another as Doctor. The conductor on the train had
evidently overheard us, and on the way to Toronto came
hurriedly into our compartment, saying that there was a
woman on the train desperately sick with a heart attack, and
asked that we would minister to her. Unfortunately we had
to confess that we were only doctors who preached, and not
those who practiced.

On our way from Toronto to Montreal, the boat put in

for a short stay at Rochester. While the boat lay there, we went to an animal exhibit which was being staged near the dock. It was late in the evening, and, as I recall, there were not many there besides Mr. Boggs and myself. The trainer was putting some lions through their paces, when one of the lions became quite rambunctious and had to be subdued with a poker, much to Mr. Boggs' alarm. In Quebec, we put up not at the stylish Hotel Frontenac, but at the St. Louis, a much less expensive place. In the middle of the night we heard the sounds of a scuffle and loud outcries, just outside our door. To defend ourselves, we pushed the heavy eighteenth-century bed up against the door. When we left the room in the morning, we saw all about the wall, and at the door of the elevator, stains of blood. It turned out that a man suffering from delirium tremens had been ejected from the hotel.

We travelled through the Evangeline country, and then across the Bay of Fundy to Digby, where we saw the vast reach of the Bay of Fundy tide. Our next adventure was at Halifax, Nova Scotia. The large room which we occupied in the hotel opened directly upon the harbor. In the middle of the night we both awakened, hearing the sounds of bells and sirens, and both had the impression that our hotel was on fire. We leaped out of bed, ran to the window, and were ready, if necessary, to leap into the sea; but by the time we got our heads out of the window we realized that there was no occasion for alarm.

Our tickets took us home by ship from Halifax to Boston; but Mr. Boggs had become seasick when we crossed the Bay of Fundy, and declared that he would not go on the ship to Boston. We therefore had to go by train, and this additional expense completely exhausted our funds. Mr. Boggs knew of a family in his church who were to visit Boston about that time, and thought he could get assistance from them;

but we discovered that they had sailed for Philadelphia the day before. Then I happened to remember a man named Deitrich. Fred Deitrich had been a student at Geneva College, and I remembered him well, partly because he had a wooden leg. In Boston he had practiced law and had been elected to the legislature. I looked in the telephone book and found where his offices were. All day we hung about that building, waiting for a man with a wooden leg to appear and deliver us out of our distress. At length, in the late afternoon, he came to his office. He could not remember me, for I was but a child when he was at Geneva College; but he knew the name well, and on the strength of the family name, cashed a check for us, and thus we were able to buy tickets for Philadelphia. It was one of those trips where the truth was stranger than fiction.

Six years after I went to Paterson my father died, in September, 1911. His last public appearance was in the previous June, when he took part in the installation of my brother Albert at the Kenwood Church in Chicago. On that occasion I preached the sermon and Father was to make the installation prayer. When I was well along toward the conclusion of the sermon, Father, who had been sitting in the body of the church, arose from his pew and came slowly down the aisle to the pulpit. He evidently thought that I was, or ought to be, at the end of my sermon. Needless to say, the whole interest of the congregation was at once centered in the venerable patriarch as he walked in his stately manner down the aisle, and not upon what I was saying. That summer he took to his bed and seldom left it. The other two sons were far away in the West, but Albert and I were frequently home during that summer. In mid-September I went to Beaver Falls after my Sunday night service at Paterson. On Friday night, bag in hand, I was coming down the stairs to start for the station to take the train back to New

Jersey. Half way down I stopped. Something seemed to say to me, "Wait; don't go tonight." I turned and carried my bag back to my room. Within an hour, and while the Old College bell was ringing for the meeting of the Friday night literary societies, Father died. He was buried from the chapel of the College, two of his oldest friends and associates, Dr. H. H. George and Dr. William Pollock Johnston, taking part in the service.

At what seemed then, but would not seem so today, an early age, sixty, he had retired from his post at Geneva College, and, except for a year with the American Sabbath Association, was never again in active work. His chief contribution in life was the part he took in establishing and maintaining Geneva College. He was a man of wide general knowledge, and in the field of science he could give sound and lucid explanations. In his early years at the College he had taken summer courses at Martha's Vineyard under the great biologist, Louis Agassiz. Father was always a strong opponent of the evolutionary hypothesis. I never had much grounding in that field of science, but the fact that Father, with his considerable study in that field, and his sound common sense, always denied the truth of the Darwinian theory, has led me to doubt that theory myself.

He was a great companion to his children. I can see him with the handkerchief over his eyes, and his hands spread out, as he joined us after dinner in the dining room for a game of Blind Man's Buff. When he was well on toward seventy, he took a hard river outing with us up to Beaver. I never knew him to be impatient or angry, save on one occasion, when Billy, our family horse, was slow and reluctant about getting into the shafts which Father was holding up for him, and to hasten his movements, he gave him a prodigious kick in the belly. Those who had heard him as a young man said that when he was lifted up he was a powerful and impressive preacher. He had a memoriter system all his own, a series of numerals, line after line, on a sheet of paper, but he could never explain to us how his system worked. In the pulpit it was as a pleader at the Throne of Grace, rather than as a preacher, that he excelled. All who remembered him in the pulpit spoke of his prayers. He had a way of weaving into his intercessions and supplications the sublime sentences of David, Jeremiah, Isaiah and St. Paul. In person he was handsome, dignified and impressive. When I think of him and his life and influence, I say to myself, in the words of the Psalmist, "My father's God, and I will exalt Him."

CHAPTER XV

PHILADELPHIA

DURING the years I was at Paterson I received three important, but totally unsolicited, calls to churches in other cities, the First Church of Lancaster, Pennsylvania, the Central Church of Wilmington, Delaware, and the South Church of Syracuse, New York. All of these churches were, in a way, stronger than the First Church of Paterson; but when the time came to decide, I chose to remain in Paterson. I had secured a somewhat unique place in the city, and took a pardonable pride in holding large congregations in a church whose property a few years before had been on the market. Then there was the pull of the heart, the close and abiding friendships which had been formed. In declining these calls I was not unmindful of the risk of a let-down, and the danger of looking back and regretting the decision I had made. To guard against that, I girded up my loins and fell to, harder than ever. After declining one of these calls, Syracuse, I think it was, I remember how I hired a brougham, in which I generally drove to funerals, and set out on a record number of pastoral calls.

But at length came the call which I accepted. This is the way it came about. I preached the sermon at the installa-

tion of a young man at the Second Presbyterian Church in
Paterson. Among those present was a friend of the minister
and his family, Governor Franklin Fort. The Governor
worshiped in the summer time at Spring Lake, New Jersey,
where the headquarters of the state were established in the
summer months. When the committee in charge of the sup-
plies for the pulpit at the Spring Lake Chapel were making
up its list of summer preachers, Governor Fort suggested my
name, and I preached there on a July Sabbath. About that
time the pulpit of the Arch Street Church in Philadelphia
became vacant. One of the elders went to see Mr. William
H. Scott, a well-known Philadelphia printer, to submit to
him some names which had been suggested for the Arch
Street pulpit. Mr. Scott, who had heard me the summer before in the Spring Lake Church, looked over the list of names,
and then said, "Dismiss all of them. Here is the man for
you," and gave him my name. Thus, by apparent chance
and little happenings is our destiny in life worked out.

On an October Sabbath I stopped at Philadelphia on
my way home from a visit to my mother at Beaver Falls, and
preached at the Arch Street Church. My breath was almost
taken away when I went up the high steps, past the big Cor-
inthian pillars, and stood under the great dome of that beautiful sanctuary. "What a place to preach!" I thought to myself. In due season I received a unanimous call, and, in contrast with the three previous calls to churches which presented
no such problem as the Arch Street Church, I felt from the
first that this was the place for me. The position of the
church, in the very heart of one of America's greatest and
oldest cities, made a strong appeal to me. There were indeed many difficulties and problems. The church was much
run down, the congregation sparse; it was on the "wrong
side" of Market Street, and most of the brown stone mansions
along Arch Street had already become rooming houses. One

Philadelphia preacher, when he heard of the call and my acceptance of it, said, "He is digging his grave!" But incomparable youth sees only the opportunity, and laughs at the obstacles. I felt that a "great door and effectual" had been opened for me. If indeed it was a grave I was digging, then truly I could say, in the words I have quoted so often in the cemeteries, "Blessed are the dead who die in the Lord."

The congregation, though small, had in its membership some of the highest types of Presbyterians, intelligent, faithful and devoted to the church: the Deal sisters, the Pattons, the Palmers, the Stevensons, and the elect Lady, Mrs. Julia M. Turner. These people needed no exhortation to attend the Sunday night and the Wednesday night services, for they were always present. It was not a Sunday morning or Communion Sabbath Session, for the elders attended regularly all the services. Mrs. Turner, of Cotton Mather descent, lived in one of the fine old mansions on Walnut Street. She never owned an automobile, always driving to church in a hired brougham; yet probably no woman in all the Presbyterian church made a larger investment in the missionary work of the church, supporting missionaries, and putting up schools and hospitals in all parts of the world. With her in the pew sat the three Deal sisters, Seraph, Sarah, and Emily. They were highly cultivated women, devout, and very generous. They were ardent premillenialists, and looked for the imminent coming of the Lord. I think they expected, at least hoped, as indeed all Christians ought to hope, that the Lord would come in their own lifetime; and when one of them died, and the Lord still tarried, it was a shock to the remaining two. After I went to the First Church at Pittsburgh, these three sisters gave to Geneva College, as a token of their friendship for me, the splendid Clarence Edward Macartney Library.

Another personality in the congregation, and a true pillar of the church, was the banker, George Stevenson. He was slightly lame, dragging one foot a little, and, as he came down the aisle with his gold-headed cane in his hand and opened the door to his pew, he would blow out his cheek with a puff that could be heard up and down the aisle. After the service he always stood at the high table before the pulpit, counting the offering with two other trustees, Mr. Palmer and Dr. Long. Mr. Stevenson desired to propose my name for membership in the Union League of Philadelphia, the Gibraltar of Republicanism and political conservatism; but when he learned of me that I voted once for Bryan and once for Wilson, he said it would be unwise to present my name.

In the congregation was the family of Mr. John Woodbridge Patton. Mr. Patton had been a professor in the Law School of the University of Pennsylvania, and was a lawyer of note in the city. We became good friends, and I was often in his home and delighted greatly in his conversation and reminiscenses. He had a splendid head, both as to shape and contents. It was moving to hear this highly intellectual man humble himself before the Lord in his public prayers at the Wednesday night service. Among his sayings which remain with me was this one, "Money is that something which buys everything but happiness, and takes a man everywhere but heaven." In discussing some difficult question about God's government of the world, he once said to me, "If we could answer that, we would know as much as God."

Riding my horse one afternoon, in beautiful Fairmount Park, I came alongside another horseman and fell into conversation with him. He turned out to be Dr. Cheesman A. Herrick, president of Girard College. That was the beginning of a pleasant and helpful friendship. Dr. Herrick and his family united with the Arch Street Church, and in due time he was elected an elder of the congregation. Through all the years I was in Philadelphia we rode together several times a week in the park. Frequently we took the long ride up the Schuylkill, and then up the picturesque Wissahickan Glen as far as the inn, where we had tea and toast. Mrs. Herrick, a highly cultivated woman, was a sister of President Edmund J. James of the University of Illinois.

In the Spring of 1918 Dr. Herrick and I went down to Culpeper, Virginia, where we secured horses and set out southward, following the route of General Grant's army in the Campaign of 1864. Our first stop was at a farmhouse overlooking the Rapidan River at Germana Ford, where the army crossed into the Wilderness. The aged farmer, with whom we had cornbread and clabber, well over eighty, had never been further from home than Culpeper. He remembered clearly the day the army crossed the Ford. The weather had suddenly turned warm, and for miles the roads were strewn with the blue overcoats which the soldiers had discarded.

We spent the first night at Spottsylvania Court House, where one of the bloody Wilderness battles had been fought. The next morning, as we were riding along the rough country road through the tangles of the Wilderness, I stopped to photograph the monument of General John Sedgwick, commander of the Sixth Corps, who was killed there by a sharpshooter. Just a moment before he was killed he had rebuked a dodging soldier, saying, "They couldn't hit an elephant at that distance!" Dr. Herrick had ridden on ahead of me, and was having a talk with a rural mail postman, his horse's head right up against the postman's buckboard. That was a fortunate thing for me, for had the postman not been looking back as he talked with Dr. Herrick, the accident which befell me might not have been noticed. I had spurred up my horse to catch up with Dr. Herrick, and was just saying to myself, "I am getting some speed out of this old rack of bones," when the horse stumbled and pitched clear over on his back, with me alongside his upturned legs. He got to his feet without trampling me, and after a moment or two I too was able to arise, but with a broken arm. The postman had seen the accident, and Dr. Herrick at once rode back to assist me. With much distress I remounted and rode along until we came to an old-fashioned wooden pump by the roadside. There we dismounted, while Dr. Herrick pumped cold water on my aching arm. A little further along we stopped at a farmhouse where a Mr. Faulkner and his dark-haired, good-looking daughter lived. Quick as a flash, the daughter ripped up a sheet and made a sling for my arm. In that way I finished the long and painful ride through the Wilderness to Fredericksburg, stopping at the Chancellor House, around which the Battle of Chancellorsville raged, and where we viewed the monument to Stonewall Jackson on the spot where he was mortally wounded.

A few months after I began my work in Philadelphia, the old church began to show signs of new life. The church was redecorated within and without, and Mrs. Turner gave us a splendid new pipe organ. The pillars in front of the church were illuminated with electric lights, and signs erected for the sermon topics. I had a most efficient janitor and custodian, who went about with the window cards announcing the topics. Before him there had been a janitress, whose nephew he was, and whom he assisted in firing the several furnaces in the vast catacombs of the cellar. He had been the successful manager of a chain grocery store, but a weakness for drink was his undoing. I remember the day he came into my study, tears rolling down his cheeks, and asked me if I had a pledge he could sign. I prayed with him, and wrote out a pledge to which he signed his name. When his aunt had to give up her post I recommended him to the trustees. They were hesitant to employ him because of his known weakness for drink, but I assured them that if they gave him a chance I would keep in close touch with him and that I was confident he would make a faithful custodian. He was given the job, and so far as I know, never again lapsed into his old habits. He was a man of good address and personality, wrote a clear hand, and did some secretarial work for me as well. I rate him as one of my chief helpers in the work in Philadelphia. His comments on the sermon were always worth while, and I knew that if the sermon pleased and interested him, I was "getting it across."

Not far from the Arch Street Church were several medical schools, Hahneman, the Medico Chirurgical, Jefferson, and somewhat farther off, Temple, and the University of Pennsylvania. I made a strong effort to reach these medical students, traditionally the hardest of all to reach, and was not altogether unsuccessful. I had special cards made out and mailed them to all the students whose names I could get. It was at one of those October services for medical students that I first preached my sermon, "Come Before Winter." There was a large congregation of medical students present. The next day I received a postal card from one of them expressing his high appreciation of the sermon. He was Hilton Wick of New Bethlehem, Pennsylvania, and who in that town practiced his profession for many years, following in the footsteps of his father and grandfather.

Another student present was a young man from New Galilee, Pennsylvania, Arnot Walker. When he came down the aisle after the service and out into the street with the rest of the students, that beautiful text, "Come Before Winter," kept echoing in his ears. He went up Arch Street to his boarding house and sat down in his room to read a magazine. But still the text kept sounding in his mind, and laying aside the magazine, he said to himself, "I think I had better write a letter to mother." When the letter was finished, a letter such as every mother delights to receive from her son, he went down to the corner and dropped it in the mailbox. A few days later he was handed a yellow envelope of the Western Union. Tearing it open, he read, "Come home at once, mother dying."

He took the night train to Pittsburgh, then another train to New Galilee, where a brother met him and drove him rapidly to his farm home. Up the stairs he hurried and into his mother's room, and was in time to see a smile of joy on his mother's face, which if a man has once seen he can never forget till "with the morn those angel faces smile which we have loved long since and lost awhile." And there under his mother's pillow was the letter he had written her on Sunday night, her viaticum, her heart's ease, as she went down in the cold waters of death's river. When he met me on the street in Philadelphia, a few days later, he said, "I am glad you preached that sermon, Come Before Winter." This, and the postcard I had received from the other student, Hilton Wick, suggested to me the wisdom of preaching a sermon on that text every autumn. The sermon was first preached on October 10, 1915. Every autumn since, I have preached on the same text, and always to a great congregation, and never without encouraging reaction. One card I received read, "Be sure and give us Come Before Winter. We missed it last year." The card was signed, "A Rounder." On the thirtieth anniversary of its first preaching, the sermon was published as a booklet. Since first preaching the sermon, I have often seen the topic and text announced by other preachers. Whether they gave me credit for the suggestion, or for the sermon, I know not; but I rejoice that, even in that way, the message of the preciousness of passing opportunity has been spread abroad.

Wherever I go to preach I generally am greeted by some doctor who worshiped at the Arch Street Church when a student in Philadelphia. After preaching recently at the Assembly Hall at Montreat, North Carolina, a doctor, a distinguished surgeon from Charlotte, came up to speak with me. He said he had seen in the papers that I was going to preach, and had driven over all the way from Charlotte to hear me. He then went on to say that one night when he was a medical student at the University of Pennsylvania I came to call at the fraternity house to which he belonged. They were staging an amateur prizefight when I arrived, and no doubt there was a little embarrassment on both sides. I talked with them for a little, and then went on my way. But the next Sunday this student came down to the Arch Street Church and attended regularly all the years he was at the University, although I never got to know him. He spoke in a most encouraging way of the debt he owed to those Sunday night services, and the influence they had exerted on his life. I had no recollection of the call at the fraternity house that night. Here again that text came back to me, that great assurance for the preacher, "Cast thy bread upon the waters, for thou shalt find it after many days."

The first summer I was in Philadelphia, in company with my brother Albert and my mother, I took a trip to England and Scotland. When off the coast of Wales, the channel squadron of the British navy sailed past us. Winston Churchill, First Lord of the Admiralty, had wisely seen to it that the navy was in readiness for the war which soon broke out. We got word of the assassination of the Austrian Crown Prince at Sarajevo when we were at sea. We landed at Plymouth, visited Exeter Cathedral, and went on to Tintagel, with its memories of King Arthur. On Sunday we worshiped in the little church near the cliffs, with the spray of the waves rolling clear in from Labrador driving over the church. The rector, evidently ill, and with a towel wound around his neck, preached a six-minute sermon. But in it he said something worth remembering, that we do not really worship God unless we sincerely desire to become what He would like us to be.

From Tintagel we went down to quaint Clovelly, in Devon, and over to Morwenstow in Cornwall, where we visited the church of which the celebrated Robert S. Hawker had been the vicar. He was a very gifted, as well as very eccentric, man. On his pastoral rounds he was accompanied by a devoted pig. When he married a couple he would always toss the ring into the air before giving it to the groom to place on the bride's finger. When asked about this, he said it was because marriage was a "toss up." He was the author of many poems including the powerful "The Quest of the Sangraal." In his peom "Morwennae Statio" are these noble lines, which can well be spoken of any venerable church of the Christian faith:

> *The very ground with speech is fraught,*
> *The air is eloquent of God.*
> *In vain would doubt or mockery hide*
> *The buried echoes of the past;*
> *A voice of strength, a voice of pride,*
> *Here dwells within the storm and blast.*
>
> *Still points the tower, and pleads the bell;*
> *The solemn arches breathe in stone;*
> *Window and wall have lips to tell*
> *The mighty faith of days unknown.*
> *Yea! flood, and breeze, and battle shock*
> *Still beat upon the church in vain;*
> *She stands, a daughter of the rock,*
> *The changeless God's eternal fane.*

From Clovelly we went by boat to Ilfracombe. That night my brother and I walked along the esplanade and

paused to listen to the music of a band. When they had concluded a number, I remarked to my brother, "That's certainly a catchy air." In a few weeks it was sung by thousands of British soldiers going into battle. The song was,
"It's a Long Way to Tipperary."

When we reached London there was some talk of war,
yet none seemed to feel that it was really imminent. But
two weeks later, when my brother and I came out of the
service at St. George's Church in Edinburgh, where we heard
Dr. John Kelman preach, newspapers telling of England's
ultimatum to Germany were being sold in front of the
church. This let us know that war was near. Those were the
first newspapers ever sold in Scotland on the Sabbath day.
The war came when we were at Newtonmore, in the Highlands. We went to the little station to see the boys from
the village off for the front. Most of them never returned.
I remember the soft weeping of the mothers and sisters as
they waved goodbye to their sons and brothers. There were
rumors that Russian troops were being shipped through
Scotland and England to the front in France, and several
times we went down to the station to take a look at these
legendary Russians.

When we returned from the Highlands we went out to
Blairbeth, my mother's still-beautiful country home, five
miles out from Glasgow. She had often told us how with
unfailing regularity the wrens returned every year and built
their nests at the well between the house and the stables.
When we walked around the house to the well, the wrens
were still there. But the noble master of the house, John
Robertson, and his wife, and the sons and daughters, were
all gone. We went down to the Isle of Bute, too, where my
grandfather had his first mill, where my mother was born,
and where on that eventful Sabbath, looking up into the pulpit of the church, she first saw the face of my father. We

sailed for home on the Anchor liner Columbia, much crowded with American tourists who had been caught in the outbreak of war. The cabin windows were darkened at night; but we took that to be a precaution against possible capture by a German cruiser. None imagined then that German submarines would sink a passenger ship; but in a few months the fate of the *Lusitania* opened the eyes of the world. The first World War now seems to us a far different war than the second. There were stories of German atrocities, how men were crucified to barns, and so on; but nothing comparable to the mass annihilations of World War II. Moreover, America was in the war for only a little more than a year.

While the war lasted, it was, for us at least, a "singing" war. How the soldiers and everybody else sang, "There's a Long, Long Trail A'winding," "Tipperary," and "Over There!" But in World War II there was little singing. Woodrow Wilson made his "Too Proud to Fight" speech in Philadelphia, and in the Presidential campaign of 1916 the Democratic slogan was, "He Kept Us Out of War." Late on the night of the election I saw the members of the Union League pouring boisterously out of their club house on Broad Street as they started a victory parade. The parade, however, was premature, for by the next night we knew that Hughes had been defeated and that Wilson was re-elected. In a few months everyone was cheering the President "who kept us out of war" for leading us into war. I heard Hughes speak during the 1916 campaign. He inspired respect, but he was anything but a spellbinder on the stump, and probably it would have been good policy for the Republican managers to keep him at home. The large vote he received was a tribute to the high regard in which he was held, and to his record as Governor of New York and as a Justice of the Supreme Court. The campaign was a contest between two ministers' sons, Hughes, the son of a Baptist, and Wilson, the son of a Presbyterian minister. Never before or since, perhaps, in the history of the country have two such able and superior men, both as to character, heredity, intellect and ability, opposed one another in a presidential campaign.

On one of my trips to England, when looking about in one of the old book stores in Paternoster Row, under the shadow of St. Paul's Cathedral, I came upon a little two-penny pamphlet, "Christianity and Common Sense." I do not recall the name of the author, but it was a defense of the cardinal doctrines of the Christian faith on the ground of common sense; that is, that the experience and intuitions of mankind are all on the side of Christian faith. This suggested to me a series of sermons of an apologetic nature, but popular in form. I tried it first in Paterson, and then in Philadelphia. Through this long doctrinal series in Philadelphia, and when I frequently preached for an hour, the large Sunday night congregations filled the church. In Pittsburgh I worked along the same line, this time preaching the sermons in the form of a dialogue between a believer and a doubter. I called it "The Doubter's Dialogue." The series commanded a great hearing. It was, however, a difficult form of preaching, for in that dialogue, where I took the part of both the believer and the doubter, there could be no hesitation, and no confusion of the "Spirit of Doubt" with the "Believer." My experience in this field of preaching convinced me anew that there is nothing so interesting to the great number of people as the great doctrines of the Christian faith, and nothing which comes closer to men's hearts and consciences. Take, for example, the doctrine of Predestination. I have never announced that I would preach on that lofty theme when there was not present on a Sunday night a large congregation. Things happen to people, and they wonder why they happen. A man who preaches on the great doctrines is preaching, not only to the times, but to the eternities.

A few years after I went to the Arch Street Church in Philadelphia, the radio became a practical reality. The Arch Street Church was one of the first to broadcast its services. When a generous friend proposed that we put the services at Arch Street on the air, I had considerable misgivings. It seemed to me that it would cheapen the message of the church and put it on a level with secular entertainment. But at length the experiment was made. I was amazed at the reaction. Letters poured in in shoals, and there were not wanting evidences that God was blessing the radio sermon and the service. What struck me particularly was the frequent comment on the pulpit prayers. People who were invalids, or had fallen away from the church, or who had never gone to church at all, seemed to be more moved by the prayers than by the sermon. I received so many letters that I resolved to announce a week-night meeting in the church for radio listeners only, when they would have an opportunity to testify as to the help which the broadcast sermons had brought them. It was "drawing a bow at a venture," but the church was crowded with all kinds of people, and, when the ice was broken, the testimonies began to follow fast one upon another as in one of the old "Experience Meetings."

One night long after, when I was in Pittsburgh, I was getting on a train at Hot Springs, Virginia, to return to Pittsburgh, when I fell into conversation with a Catholic priest from Philadelphia. When he learned my name he told me that when I was preaching on the radio during the great theological controversy over the fundamental truths of the Christian faith, the rector of the parish where he served would gather all the clergy together on Sunday nights to listen to my sermons on the great Christian doctrines. He told me, too, that some of the priests at St. Charles Borromeo, the Catholic theological seminary at Overbrook, on the outskirts of Philadelphia, also frequently listened to these sermons. While we deplore what to us Protestants seems like idolatry in Roman Catholic worship, nevertheless, when it comes to the fundamental truths of the Christian faith, a believing Protestant and a Roman Catholic can stand shoulder to shoulder. There is between them much more real fellowship than between a Protestant evangelical and a Protestant modernist.

CHAPTER XVI

FOR THE FAITH

IN 1922 Dr. Harry Emerson Fosdick, a Baptist clergyman, was the guest preacher and stated supply at the First Presbyterian Church of New York City. He preached one Sunday morning on the subject, "Shall the Fundamentalists Win?" The sermon, but not at his suggstion, was put into pamphlet form and circulated throughout the land by a publicity agent of the Rockefeller Foundation, a Mr. Ivy Lee.

I think this was the first time I had ever seen or heard the word "Fundamentalist" used in a religious significance. There was some association of ministers and laymen pledged to the defense of the great doctrines of the Gospel, who had put out a series of pamphlets on "The Fundamentals: A Testimony to the Truth." That is how the name "Fundamentalist" arose. It was a word tossed about with a great deal of scorn and contempt on the part of the modernists during the great discussions over basic Christian truth; but since everyone believes in foundations, "Fundamentalist" was not, after all, a bad name. Most of the principles which the so-called "Fundamentalists" emphasized were accepted by the great majority of Protestants, and are embodied in the creeds of all the evangelical churches, and the

Roman Catholic too; such as the infallibility of the Bible, the virgin birth, the vicarious atonement, the bodily resurrection of Christ, and His second advent. The only difference between the "Fundamentalists" and the great body of conservative and evangelical believers lay in the fact that, while all true Christians believe that Christ will come again in glory and in judgment, the "Fundamentalists" held to a premillennial and imminent coming of Christ.

I had had no association with any so-called "Fundamentalist" group; but when I read Dr. Fosdick's sermon, "Shall the Fundamentalists Win?" it struck me as a direct assault upon cardinal Christian truth. In his sermon Dr. Fosdick said, for example, speaking of the virgin birth of Jesus as related in the gospels of St. Matthew and St. Luke:

"To believe in virgin birth as an explanation of great personality is one of the familiar ways in which the ancient world was accustomed to account for unusual superiority. . . . Those first disciples adored Jesus—as we do; when they thought about his coming they were sure he came specially from God—as we are; this adoration and conviction they associated with God's special influence and intention in his birth—as we do; but they phrased it in terms of a biological miracle that our modern minds cannot use."

This extraordinary sermon I answered with one entitled, "Shall Unbelief Win?" This sermon, too, was printed in pamphlet form and widely circulated. It at once evoked strong comments, most of them commendatory, some very hostile and scornful. In October of that year, 1922, the Presbytery of Philadelphia met at the beautiful estate of John Wanamaker at Jenkintown. In the course of the meeting I arose and requested an executive session, which meant that all non-members of the Presbytery, and visitors and reporters, must leave the room. Then I introduced an Address to the Presbytery of New York from the Presbytery of Phila-

delphia, asking the Presbytery of New York to see to it that
the preaching in the pulpit of the First Church be in conformity with the standards of the Presbyterian Church.
There was no little excitement and considerable heated discussion, after which I yielded to the request that action be
postponed until the next meeting, and that a copy of the Address to the Presbytery of New York be mailed to every member. At the next meeting of the Presbytery an overture was
adopted and forwarded to the Clerk of the General Assembly. This overture, in substance the Address which I had
framed to the Presbytery of New York, requested the
General Assembly to see to it that the preaching in the First
Church of New York be in conformity with the doctrines of
the Presbyterian Church as set forth in the Confession of
Faith.

The introduction of this overture caused a mighty stir,
partly because of the prominence and popularity of Dr. Fosdick. This popularity was due not only to his remarkable
gifts of expression and high ability as a preacher, but also to
the fact that he was voicing and defending sub-Scriptural
views of Christ and the Gospel which were already in the
minds of thousands of people.

The newspapers of New York and other great cities
gave the matter extraordinary publicity. Mass meetings of
conservative and evangelical Presbyterians were held in
different centers, and the battle raged in all parts of the
church. I sounded out some of those who were reputed to be
leaders in the Presbyterian Church as to their reaction to
what I had done. Some, like Henry Van Dyke of Princeton
University, were openly scornful. Others sidestepped the
issue, quite evidently fearing to commit themselves, lest
someone should label them as "Fundamentalists." One
prominent Washington minister said I was trying to do the
work that Christ had appointed for the angels, referring to

the parable of the wheat and the tares, in which Jesus said to let the tares grow together with the wheat until the harvest, when the angels would gather up the tares and cast them into the furnace.

I had expected, of course, criticism and scoffing, and that the old cry and accusation, "heresy hunter," would go up. But what surprised me was the intemperate and bitter abuse which poured forth. At the meeting of the Presbytery when the overture was adopted, I thought for a moment that one of the Presbyters was going to make a physical assault upon me. The letters of abuse poured in like a flood. I have preserved these letters in my files, and I call them, the "Liturgy of Execration." The so-called Liberals and Modernists certainly did not live up to their vaunted reputation and their claim of "sweetness and light."

The big disappointment in the whole matter was Princeton Theological Seminary. The Philadelphia overture was only defending what Princeton had taught us; but when I wrote to certain members of the faculty I was shocked and disappointed at the way in which they sidestepped the issue and avoided committing themselves on the overture. However, the majority of the faculty were with us, notably, Dr. William Brenton Greene, Jr., professor of apologetics, Dr. Robert Dick Wilson, the noted Old Testament scholar, and my two classmates, Dr. Oswald T. Allis of the Old Testament department, and Dr. J. Gresham Machen of the New Testament department. Dr. Machen came out like a lion at the very beginning of the battle.

Perhaps this is as good a place as any to say a word about a remarkable personality, Dr. Machen. He came of a well-known Baltimore family, where his father was a noted lawyer and his mother an "elect lady" in faith and in intellect. Chiefly through the influence of his pastor at the Franklin Street Presbyterian Church, Dr. Harris E. Kirk, between whom and Dr. Machen, unfortunately, there afterwards arose an aloofness and coolness, he entered Princeton Theological Seminary, where his unusual talent was at once recognized. After graduating at Princeton he studied at the Universities of Marburg and Göttingen in Germany and returned to Princeton as an assistant in the New Testament department. Both as a student and as a professor, Dr. Machen was known, not only as a scholar, but as a "stunter." At student gatherings he would get off an amusing recitation about "Old Bill" and Napoleon. None thought of him then, as his modernist foes afterwards caricatured him, as sour, bitter and unfriendly.

The moment the Fosdick issue was raised, Dr. Machen threw himself, with his learning, talent, zeal, social standing and wealth, into the battle. During the course of the controversy which followed, Dr. Machen was elected to the Chair of Apologetics at Princeton Seminary. Then his enemies, and the enemies of the truth which he represented and defended, got busy and blocked his confirmation as a professor at the Baltimore General Assembly of 1926. Both Dr. Machen's friends and his enemies knew that no one in the whole country was better qualified for the Chair of Apologetics; but he was the target of abuse because of his uncompromising stand on the great issue before the church. The fact that his brother Arthur was head of the Anti-Prohibition Society, and that Dr. Machen himself did not favor what was called "sumptuary" legislation, was played up against him, until one would have thought that the real issue was not the truth of the Bible, the vicarious atonement, the virgin birth and the resurrection, but Prohibition. I myself lamented Dr. Machen's stand on that issue; but I did not permit this to blind me to his magnificent witness to the great truths of the Gospel.

In 1929 Dr. Machen led a seceding group of professors

and students from Princeton and founded Westminster Theological Seminary at Philadelphia. The seminary prospered from the very beginning. Although I was one of the few on the old Board of Directors at Princeton who were not ousted when the General Assembly reorganized the Board in 1929, I withdrew from Princeton and became a Director of the new seminary at Philadelphia, and made the address at the first commencement. The seminary had all the students it could care for, and sufficient funds came in from rich and poor all over the world. Since men graduating from sub-orthodox and non-Presbyterian seminaries, such as Union and Yale, were continually being licensed and ordained by the Presbyteries, no hindrance could be put in the way of the graduates of such a truly Presbyterian seminary as Westminster. Thus the seminary was quickly fulfilling the purpose for which it had been founded. That was to pour a stream of evangelical belief and teaching into the Presbyterian ministry.

Then came the cloud on the horizon. Dr. Machen and a few others organized the Independent Board for Presbyterian Foreign Missions. If he had named it the Independent Board for Foreign Missions, or the Evangelical Board for Foreign Missions, or some similar name, the result might have been different. But when he called it the Independent Board for Presbyterian Foreign Missions he gave his enemies an opening of which they at once availed themselves. The General Assembly declared this Board to be schismatic, and ordered all members of the Board who were Presbyterians to withdraw from it or stand trial. This, in my judgment, was a most unjust action. A few members did obey the Assembly and withdrew; but Dr. Machen refused to obey the mandate. He was duly tried and put out of the church. His expulsion was, as I see it, one of the darkest blots on the history of the Presbyterian Church. The fact that, in the end, this act of expulsion only exalted Dr. Machen to new heights, does not take away from the shame of it.

When Dr. Machen's trial came up before the Judicial Commission, I wrote to him, offering him my services as counsel. He replied with a kind letter, but declined my offer, saying that if I defended him, he might be acquitted, and that was not what he wanted. He had already made up his mind to secede, and promptly did so, establishing the Orthodox Presbyterian Church. The movement was abortive. Only a handful of men, sincere and courageous, however, followed Dr. Machen in the secession. Dr. Machen died in 1937 in Bismarck, North Dakota, where he had gone to assist the pastor of the Orthodox Presbyterian Church. His death seemed to his friends untimely. And yet, in another sense, it was not untimely, for he was "taken away from the evil to come." Had he lived, he would have seen the seminary which he founded split with faction, and the Board of Missions and the Orthodox Church which he established falling far short of what he had planned and expected. His true monument is not in these institutions or societies, but in the inspiration he left behind him of his courageous, devout and highly intellectual witness to the "grand particularities" of the Christian faith. His two masterly books, *The Origin of Paul's Religion,* and *The Virgin Birth,* will long remain classics in that field of theology. When I think of Dr. Machen, I think of that tradition about Thomas Aquinas, how Christ appeared unto him and said, "Thomas, thou hast spoken well of me. Now what wilt thou have?" "Thyself, Lord," was the answer of the great schoolman. Dr. Machen spoke and wrote "well" of his Lord. We doubt not that now he knows and experiences that greatest of all gifts and rewards, "Thyself, Lord." What Beza said at the

189

end of his brief, but most admirable, biography of John Calvin, can truly be said of Dr. Machen— "An example which it is as easy to slander as it is difficult to imitate."

The General Assembly of 1923 met in Indianapolis. Just before this meeting I was elected Moderator of the Presbytery of Philadelphia, and led a delegation of truly conservative Commissioners to the Assembly. William Jennings Bryan was nominated for the moderatorship, but was defeated by Dr. Charles Wishart, president of the College of Wooster. The Philadelphia overture, asking that the Presbytery of New York see to it that the preaching in the pulpit of the First Church of that city be in conformity with the standards of the church, was, in due process, referred to the Committee on Bills and Overtures. The chairman was the Rev. Hugh K. Walker. Nolan R. Best, the editor of "The Continent," one of the three Presbyterian weeklies, was a member of the committee. The only man on the committee about whom we could feel sure was Dr. A. Gordon MacLennan, of the Bethany Collegiate Church, Philadelphia. At length the Committee on Bills and Overtures, through the chairman, Dr. Walker, brought in its report on the Philadelphia overture. It was a weak and meaningless evasion, and tantamount to a whitewash of Dr. Fosdick and the Presbytery of New York. Yet every member of the committee signed the report—all save one, Dr. MacLennan. Those who supported the minority report of Dr. MacLennan, which carried out the purpose of the Philadelphia overture, and directed the Presbytery of New York to take action, were given an opportunity to speak. Dr. MacLennan made a powerful speech in his great booming voice, and I followed. There was an amusing interlude in this altogether dramatic and tense debate. A minister from St. Louis, who wanted to support our side, took the floor, but it was impossible to tell from what he said which side he was on, and as he spoke he kept turning to those on the platform, with his back to the Commissioners, and repeatedly had to be turned about in the other direction by the Moderator. Everybody got a good laugh out of it. Mr. Bryan then arose and demanded a roll call vote, "so that the folks back home will know how we voted." In the gathering gloom the dramatic roll took place. The minority report, or the Philadelphia overture, was carried by a considerable majority (439-359).

The so-called Modernists and Liberals were now in great alarm. Hitherto they had been permitted to "bore from within," and very little protest was made against their work. Some of their leaders drew up what was called "The Auburn Affirmation," because drawn up there, with one of the professors of the Auburn Seminary a leader in it. This affirmation was signed by more than a thousand out of the ten thousand Presbyterian ministers, and there were undoubtedly hundreds of other ministers in the church who secretly favored its ill-favored doctrines. To a great host of Presbyterians, this affirmation was a Christ-dishonoring proclamation, if ever there was one. Imagine the Christian Church establishing itself in the pagan world in the first century on the ground of such affirmations! Among these affirmations were the following:

"There is no assertion in the Scriptures that their writers were kept 'from error.' . . . We hold that the General Assembly of 1923, in asserting that 'the Holy Spirit did so inspire, guide and move the writers of the Holy Scripture as to keep them from error,' spoke without warrant of the Scriptures or of the Confession of Faith. . . .

"Furthermore, this opinion of the General Assembly attempts to commit our church to certain *theories* concerning the inspiration of the Bible, and the Incarnation, the Atonement, the Resurrection, and the Continuing Life and

Supernatural Power of our Lord Jesus Christ. . . . Some of us regard the particular *theories* contained in the deliverance of the General Assembly of 1923 as satisfactory explanations of these facts and doctrines. But we are united in believing that these are not the only *theories* allowed by the Scriptures and our standards as explanation of these facts and doctrines of our religion, and that all who hold to these facts and doctrines, whatever theories they may employ to explain them, are worthy of all confidence and fellowship."

No doubt some of the men who signed the Affirmation did so as a party measure, and did not really hold the views put forth in it. Some of the signers have since greatly regretted that they signed it. Thus the lines were drawn for the battle at the Assembly of 1924. Because of the part I had taken in the support of the Philadelphia Overture, my name was put forward by the Presbytery of Philadelphia as a candidate for the office of Moderator. The opposition put up Dr. Charles R. Erdman of Princeton Theological Seminary, for the time had not yet come in the church, although it has come now, when the Modernists could nominate and elect one of their own kith and kin to the highest office of the church.

The Assembly met that year in Grand Rapids, Michigan. Because of the theological issue, it was one of the most publicized of all our General Assemblies. A great array of newspaper correspondents were present at the press tables. Dr. Erdman was nominated for the moderatorship by Dr. John Timothy Stone of the Fourth Church, Chicago. I was nominated by William Jennings Bryan in one of his characteristic speeches. My nomination was seconded by Dr. John F. Carson of the Central Presbyterian Church, Brooklyn. I remember how Dr. Carson commenced his speech with the words from Ecclesiastes, "What can the man do that cometh after the King?" referring, of course, to the great orator who had preceded him, Mr. Bryan. I doubt if a single vote was changed by any of the speeches, able though they were, for I think that every commissioner came to the Assembly with his mind made up. In an exceedingly close vote, 464 to 446, I was elected Moderator.

When I took the platform and was handed the gavel by the retiring Moderator, Dr. Wishart, there was no little curiosity on the part of the Commissioners, especially those who knew me only by the Modernists' attacks on me, to see what kind of a man this "fire-eating" minister from Philadelphia was. I straightway relieved the tension and soon had everybody laughing and in a good humor by relating a recent dream. I dreamed that I had been elected Moderator of the General Assembly of the Presbyterian Church, and on a following night that I had been sentenced to be "hanged by the neck until dead." "The first part of the dream," I said, "has come true. No doubt there are some here who may wish that the second part also would come true."

The Fosdick matter was finally turned over to the Judicial Commission which, with Robert Young, Esq., as Moderator, brought in a report which was unsatisfactory to most of the conservative Commissioners, but which nevertheless directed the Presbytery of New York to see that Dr. Fosdick, if he continued to preach in the pulpit of the First Church in New York, subscribe to our Confession of Faith and become a minister of the Presbyterian Church. Some prominent ministers of the New York Presbytery, who themselves held views similar to those of Dr. Fosdick, importuned him to subscribe to our standards and come into the church. He of course was not willing to stultify himself in such a manner, and withdrew from the pulpit of the First Church.

In 1925 I took another trip abroad, going first to Cardiff, Wales, where I attended the sessions of the Pan Presbyterian Alliance, and delivered an address on the authority of the Scripture. This plain statement of belief in the Bible was like an apple of discord tossed onto the floor of the Assembly. I was amazed at the strong and bitter speeches in the debate which ensued, particularly on the part of the Scottish delegates. Modernism has inflicted more ghastly wounds on the body of the Scottish church than on any other Protestant body. It makes one think of that verse in Hosea, "Their drink is become sour."

That same summer I made my first trip to Rome. I had always avoided Italy and Rome on my former trips to Europe because I had heard so much about the Roman fever and other summer dangers. It was, therefore, all the greater joy for me to visit the Eternal City. As Paul put it, I had often said to myself, "I must see Rome." Now I saw it. It was a jubilee year, and a certain door, opened only every twenty-five years, now admitted one to St. Peter's. The two places that I liked best of all at Rome were the Protestant Cemetery and St. Paul's Outside The Walls. The deep shade of the Protestant Cemetery was most pleasing and grateful after the fierce glare of the Italian sun. In this beautiful cemetery are the graves of John Keats and Percy Bysshe Shelley. They sleep in one corner of the cemetery, not far from one another. These two graves will make the Protestant Cemetery at Rome forever a place of pilgrimage to those who speak the language of Shakespeare. On the grave of Shelley, who died in 1822, are the words from "The Tempest":

> *Nothing of him that doth fade*
> *But doth suffer a sea-change*
> *Into something rich and strange.*

On the grave of Keats, who died in 1821, is his own non-prophetic epitaph, "Here lies one whose name was writ in water."

Of all the churches at Rome, I liked best St. Paul's Outside The Walls. In front of the church stands a statue of St. Paul holding in his hand a sword, for St. Paul is always represented with the sword, as the gladiator of the Christian faith, whereas St. Peter is always pictured with the keys of the Church and of the Kingdom in his hand. Around the walls of this church are engraved the names of all the supposed bishops of Rome. At one end of the transept is a vast mural depicting St. Paul's conversion on the way to Damascus. According to the tradition, the dust of St. Paul reposes in the crypt of the church of St. Paul Outside The Walls. Standing there and looking down into the crypt, there came to my mind that magnificent eulogy on St. Paul by the golden-mouthed Chrysostom of Antioch:

"Would that it were now given to me to throw myself round the body of Paul, and be rivetted to the tomb, and to see the dust of that body . . . that served the gospel everywhere . . . This is the mouth, the dust whereof I would fain see, through which Christ spake the great and secret things and greater than in his own person . . . Nor is it the mouth only, but the heart too I would fain see the dust of, which a man would not do wrong to call the heart of the world . . . This heart was so large as to take in entire cities, and peoples, and nations. . . . which burned at each one that was lost. . . . which despised death and hell yet was broken down by a brother's tears. Fain would I see the dust of those hands through which the divine writings were written. . . . at the sight of which the serpent fell off into the fire. Fain would I see the dust of those eyes which were blinded gloriously, which recovered their sight again for the salvation of the world . . . I would also see the dust of

those feet, which ran through the world and were not weary
. . . This body is a wall to that City which is safer than all
towers, and than thousands of battlements."

A visit to the Catacombs will deeply move anyone who
has the least degree of Christian faith in him. These gloomy
places of sepulture, far beneath the Roman campagna, were
of double interest to me because I had written a thesis on
the Catacombs for my Master's degree at Princeton University. The inscriptions which the mourners traced in the
soft mortar with the point of the trowel, when they sealed
the tomb of their beloved dead, bring back to one the faith
and hope, and the sorrows and trials of that early Christian
age.

> *"Rudely written, yet each letter*
> *Full of hope and yet of heart-break,*
> *Full of the tender pathos of the here*
> *And the hereafter."*

Here are some of the epitaphs which I spelled out as
the guiding monk held his candle up to the wall:

"To dear Cyriacus, sweetest son, mayest thou live in the
Holy Spirit." "Regine, mayest thou live in the Lord Jesus
Christ." "Victoria, in peace and in Christ." "Alexander is
not dead but lives above the stars."

After my tour through Italy, I joined my brother Albert at Lausanne, and set out for a short trip through Germany, visiting Freiburg, the Black Forest, Heidelberg, and
Worms, with its grand monument to Martin Luther. Perhaps the two greatest monuments in the world, so far as religion is concerned, are that monument to Luther at Worms
and the monument to John Huss at Prague. After our trip
through Germany we started for fabulous Spain, going by
way of Marseilles, and stopping overnight at Nimes, where is
one of the best-preserved of the ancient Roman coliseums.

We entered Spain at Port Bou and spent the first night at Barcelona. Then came the long hot journey across Spain to noisy, broiling Madrid. The famous Prado was closed, but we saw many of the masterpieces of Velasquez and Murillo at the Escorial, that colossal church, palace, monastery and museum, where King Phillip II spent his last years, his gouty leg resting on a camp stool as he ruled a great portion of the world with a stroke of his pen. In the marble crypt below, sleep most of the kings and queens of Spain, among others, the great emperor, Charles the Fifth.

Madrid, a place of terrible heat in the summer, and of terrible noises, too, we were glad to leave behind us and go down to Toledo, picturesquely set on its rocky hill, with the River Tagus circling it like a lover's arm. Now, indeed, we felt we were in cruel, romantic, superstitious, medieval, Catholic Spain. Here were the ancient towers and arches; the inn where Cervantes lived and wrote; fountains and patios, and squares where the citizens clapped their hands for the waiter, and where the yellow tickets for the bull fights were sold. In the great cathedral, the seat of Roman Catholic authority in Spain, we saw a number of the paintings of the celebrated artist, El Greco. They were mostly unfinished sketches of the Apostles, St. John and others; just an outline, as it were, of an arm, a hand, a head. It struck me as a symbol of mortality, and immortality also, for that is about all we do in life's brief day; just a few strokes, just a shadowy and fragmentary sketch, leaving the main work unfinished. In one corner of the cathedral sleep the Cardinal Archbishops of Toledo. Above each grave is suspended the red hat of the cardinal, and on the graves of these proud Princes of the Church are the three Latin words, *Pulvis, Cines, Nihil*—Dust, Ashes, Nothing!

For several years, at the invitation of the faculty, I went up one day a week to Princeton and assisted Dr. J. Ritchie

Smith in the department of Homiletics. I read the seniors' sermons and heard them preach in the chapel. In 1925 the Directors of the Seminary elected me to the chair of Christian Ethics and Apologetics, with the thought of transferring me to the chair for which I was much better fitted, that of Homiletics. There was, of course, a certain appeal in the cloistered walks and venerable halls of Princeton; but I have never doubted that I made the right decision when I declined the chair to which I had been elected. When the time came for the final decision, I felt that I would rather preach myself than try to tell others how to preach.

In 1922 my mother died at our home, Fern Cliffe, at Beaver Falls, Pennsylvania. She had spent several winters with me at Philadelphia. Although she was almost eighty when I went to Philadelphia, her zeal had not flagged nor had the eye of her faith grown dim. On Sabbath afternoons she had a class and a tea for young men from the medical colleges. From time to time I meet some of them who attended that class, and who speak of how she used to read to them in her sweet Scottish accent, passages from Ian Maclaren's "Beside the Bonnie Briar Bush." She had also a weekday afternoon class for young mothers. At the age of eighty-three her remarkable life came to an end; but her "works do follow her." I arrived home just in time to be greeted with her old-time loving smile. It was the wish of the other brothers and of my sister that I should make the address at her funeral. Taking for my text the words of Jesus, "O woman, great is thy faith," I said, in part:

"I read through the Beatitudes and nearly all of them seem to fit her; but especially that beatitude of Jesus which is reported for us by St. Paul, how it is written, 'It is more blessed to give than to receive.' She had her Calvaries and Gethsemanes, but her long life was eminently a happy one, and one that brought happiness to others because she lived

so close to an ever flowing fountain of love. . . . The secret
of having love coming in is to have love ever going out. This
was a truth beautifully illustrated by the life of our mother.
Ever a tide of love was going out from her to others, and
therefore it was that from every quarter of the earth tides
of affection were streaming in to her.

*　　　*　　　*

"Mother's mind was of strong fibre, rich in imagination
and orderly in its reasoning. She had that analytical and
speculative, perhaps metaphysical, ability which is so com-
monly associated with the Celtic temperament. This
natural endowment had been cultivated and stimulated by the advantages of a superior education. For this
reason it was a rare privilege to discuss with her the deep
things of the Kingdom of God, for she was one who served
the Lord with her heart, her soul, her strength, and also her
mind. But she knew the place of reason, that it could only
test and examine the revelation from God, and could not
take its place, and that the world by wisdom knew not God,
never could know him. Therefore she was content to walk
by faith, and not by sight. . . . On this last visit she talked
much with me about the grounds of her assurance of salvation. I quoted for her the words of St. Paul, the ultimate and
only hope of every believer, 'Being justified by faith, we
have peace with God through Jesus Christ.' There she cast
her anchor. If we were to be accepted of God on the ground
of our character, what we have done and been, I think our
mother would have a claim second to none. But she would
have been the first to disown any such claim. Her hope was
not in her own merit, unusual though it was, as men judge
merit, but in the merits of Christ, her Saviour.

*　　　*　　　*

"How often I have heard upon her lips these lines of the old Scottish paraphrase, and heard her say how they were on her father's lips before her:

> *How bright these glorious spirits shine!*
> *Whence all their white array?*
> *How came they to the blissful seats*
> *Of everlasting day?*
>
> *Lo, these are they from sufferings great*
> *Who came to realms of light,*
> *And in the blood of Christ have washed*
> *Their robes which shone so bright.*

"There we leave her, with the company of the redeemed, and in the presence of the Lamb."

On her eighty-third birthday, Mother sent this letter to her five children:

"Tomorrow is my eighty-third birthday. How few opportunities now of glorifying God and of helping others, and especially how few my opportunities now to influence my dear, dear children and gladden and make their days a blessing on the earth.

"O Lord, I confess my shortcomings in this respect. Forgive the unused or misused opportunities of leading them closer to Jesus. Forget not, and bless the earnest efforts I did make. Hear and answer still more abundantly than in past years, the prayers I offered up for them.

"I thank Thee for the precious answers Thou hast given. I thank Thee for the love of my children so richly manifested all through the years. I thank Thee for the many friends who think of me and do me kindness.

"And now I beseech Thee, O Lord, for the days to come, be they, as naturally they will be—few—or many, to grant me more faith; more love to Thee and all men; enable me to help all who come near me by my trust and confidence in Thee, to put their trust also in Thee.

"Grant to me grace to have my 'walk and conversation' even should it be on a bed of sickness, such as to recommend the Gospel of Jesus Christ, and draw saints and sinners to Him.

"Lord, bless dear Ernest, dear Robertson, dear Mina, dear Albert and their families, and dear Clarence.

"Lord, bless me; lift up the Light of Thy countenance upon me and give me peace."

CHAPTER XVII

PITTSBURGH

DURING the years I was at Philadelphia, I received calls to the Second Presbyterian Church of St. Louis, where one of the princes of the Presbyterian Church, and a former Moderator, Dr. Samuel J. Niccolls, had just died; the Pine Street Church of Harrisburg, Pennsylvania; and the New York Avenue Church of Washington, D. C., where Dr. Wallace Radcliffe had just retired. The call to Washington made a strong appeal to me, so strong, indeed, that I at first accepted the call, but afterwards declined it. For some reason I could not bring myself, at that time, to give up the Arch Street pulpit, where God had blessed my ministry. By the waters of the Schuylkill "there were great searchings of heart"; but in the end that was the decision.

I had frequently preached in the pulpit of the historic First Presbyterian Church, Pittsburgh, when the late Dr. Maitland Alexander was the minister. And what a preacher and leader he was! One October day in 1926, Dr. Alexander called me on the telephone and asked if it would be convenient for me to exchange pulpits with him, saying it would be a favor to him if I could do so. Not knowing what was in the air, I went out to Pittsburgh and preached for him the following Sunday. A few months afterwards, Dr. Alexander, after a great pastorate of twenty-nine years, resigned. I was then given a unanimous call to the First Church, and soon accepted it. It was a hard break for me to leave Arch Street and Philadelphia. I loved the people at Arch Street, where I had passed through stirring experiences, and I loved Philadelphia, its cultivated atmosphere, its old hospitals, churches and cemeteries, its historical background, its beautiful Fairmount Park, its charming suburban country, so like England. However, there was little indecision after the call from Pittsburgh came. I began my ministry there the first Sabbath of April, 1927, preaching my first sermon on the text from St. Paul's letter to the Philippians, "Your fellowship in the Gospel from the first day until now." At that time the text was hope and prediction; now it is fulfilled history. The smoke and fog of Pittsburgh, its narrow and somewhat grimy streets, were quite a contrast to Philadelphia; but Pittsburgh always had "drive" to it, and in 1927, industry and business there were at the peak.

Although the one hundred and fiftieth anniversary of the First Church was celebrated in 1934, counting 1784, when the church was incorporated, as its beginning, the history of the church goes back to 1773, fifteen years after the fall of Fort Duquesne, when Presbyterians worshiping at the frontier post at the Point sent a request to the Presbytery of Donegal, which then took in everything west of Lancaster, to send a minister over the mountain to celebrate the Lord's Supper and catechize the people. The church had had just eight ministers in its long history. Among these were some preachers and scholars of note: Dr. Francis Herron, for forty years pastor, and the chief builder of the church; Dr. William M. Paxton, afterwards minister of the First Church of New York City, and then professor of Homiletics at Princeton Theological Seminary; Dr. Sylvester F.

Scovel, afterwards president of the College of Wooster; Dr. George T. Purves, afterwards professor of the New Testament at Princeton Seminary, and then minister of the Fifth Avenue Church, New York City; Dr. David R. Breed, for many years professor of Homiletics at Western Theological Seminary, and Dr. Maitland Alexander.

Dr. Alexander was a remarkable and many-talented man. He was the grandson of the celebrated Dr. Archibald Alexander, the first professor of Princeton Seminary, and the great-grandson of James Waddel, the famous blind preacher of Augusta County, Virginia, and whose moving eloquence is described in a classic essay by the Virginia orator, William Wirt. It was in that sermon which William Wirt heard on a sacramental Sabbath that Waddel spoke the oft-quoted sentence, "Socrates died like a philosopher; Jesus died like a God." On his mother's side, Dr. Alexander was the grandson of another distinguished educator and minister, Dr. Matthew Brown, president of Jefferson College. At the Sesqui-centennial celebration of the founding of the First Church, I thus spoke of the personality and work of Dr. Alexander:

"Born to lead, Dr. Alexander would have been a success in almost every field of human endeavor and activity. In him was the rare combination of administrative genius, quick intellect, distinguished pulpit ability, and magnetic personality. Noting the changes which were coming over Pittsburgh, and the retreat of the membership of the church to the suburbs, Dr. Alexander planned for the future. He had the vision of what we see today, the First Church standing in the midst of the great city and proclaiming the everlasting gospel to the multitudes who come and go. Under his inspiring leadership, the property on Wood Street was leased and the present noble structure erected. The church was dedicated in April, 1905. Here Dr. Alexander ministered to enthusiastic congregations for twenty-nine years. Under his pastorate were inaugurated those many activities through which the First Church has touched such a multitude of lives. Among these activities are the Mother's Club, the Thursday Noon Club, the Thursday and Friday Night Girls' Clubs, the Tuesday Sewing, the Boys' Club, the work of the Church Missionary and the Church Nurse, and the Korean Club.

"In 1914 Dr. Alexander was honored by being elected to the highest post in the Presbyterian Church, the Moderator of the General Assembly. Dr. Alexander resigned his pastorate amid universal regret in the congregation, and in the city, in 1927. 'If you would see his monument, look around you.'

"Dr. Alexander's message is well summed up in the charge he gave to the congregation at the dedication of the Mary McMasters Jones preaching pulpit. Looking to the future, Dr. Alexander said:

'I charge you, the members of this Church, to see to it that when my work has been finished in this Church, that no man shall ever stand here as its minister who does not believe in and preach an inspired and infallible Bible, a living Christ who is God, and the Cross and shed Blood, the only way of everlasting life. Let no graces of speech, executive ability or power, charm of diction or literary equipment, obscure the paramount qualification for a minister of this Church, namely that he shall be true to the Bible, to all the standards of the Presbyterian Church, to the Deity of God's only Begotten Son, and Salvation through His Precious Blood alone.' "

A stirring feature of the worship of the First Church, remarked by all visitors, is the general and enthusiastic congregational singing. Perhaps the chief secret of that was the leadership of the organist, Mr. John A. Bell. Mr. Bell knew how to lead so as to make a congregation sing. At the Sesqui-centennial commemoration, Mr. Bell celebrated his fiftieth anniversary at the console. The congregation presented him with a gift, and the University of Pittsburgh with an honorary degree. The next year both he and Mrs. Bell met their death in a tragic accident near Greensburg, Pennsylvania. They "were lovely and pleasant in their lives, and in their death they were not divided." In the passing of Mr. Bell, the First Church lost a great organist and musician and a faithful elder, and I lost a chief friend and companion.

Almost everything of importance in Pittsburgh, religious and educational, had its beginning at the First Church: seminaries and cemeteries, academies and colleges, Christian Associations and patriotic societies. The church stands in the very heart of the business district of the city, and also at the very heart of the history of the city. When I began my ministry at Pittsburgh I worked in the pulpit along the same line which had been tested out in Paterson and Philadelphia, preaching series of sermons, doctrinal, biographical, and Sermons From Life. Many of these series are embodied in my books. One of the most popular in these series was the doctrinal series, "The Doubter's Dialogue," (published under the title, *Christianity and Common Sense*); also a series on the women of the Bible, "The Way of a Man with a Maid." These series were all preached at the evening service. What stirring services those were: the crowded church, the wonderful singing, the people, young and old, rich and poor, coming from all parts of the city and from the adjoining towns.

In front of the First Church, looking down on Sixth Avenue, is a richly carved Geneva pulpit. I determined to make this pulpit something more than an architectural ornament, and frequently, when the weather was favorable, conducted an outdoor service from the street pulpit for half an hour before the evening worship. Thus wisdom, as the Book of Proverbs puts it,—not my wisdom, but the Wisdom of the Word of God—"uttereth her voice in the streets."

During World War II, we made use of the street pulpit for patriotic gatherings. Citizens of Pittsburgh will not soon forget the services held from the street pulpit on D-Day, 1944, when the allied armies landed in Normandy, and on VE Day, 1945, when word came of the surrender of Germany. On that occasion I spoke as follows:

"Eleven months ago, we assembled here in front of this street pulpit to thank God on D-Day for the successful landing of the Allied Armies on the shores of France. Today we assemble here to celebrate that for which that landing last June was made, the day of complete and overwhelming victory. This is the day for which we have long waited and hoped and prayed, the day for which millions of our young men have fought, and for which thousands of them have died.

"The Saviour of mankind said, 'They that take the sword shall perish by the sword.' Five and a half years ago Germany drew the sword upon a peaceful world. That sword flashed with threat and terror and cruelty over all the world. It dripped with the blood of Poland, Norway, Denmark, Russia, Belgium, Holland, France, England, Yugoslavia, Greece, and the islands of the Mediterranean. No arm seemed powerful enough to stay and turn back that terrible sword. But now that sword, snatched from the hand that drew it, has beaten Germany into the dust. They that took the sword have perished by the sword. 'It is the Lord's doing and it is marvelous in our eyes.'

"We salute this day our great Allies, Britain and Russia, our great military leaders, General Eisenhower and his lieutenants; and reverently and prayerfully we pause to salute the dead, those 'who loved not their life unto the death.' We salute their mothers and fathers who sent them forth, and we pray that today some ray of cheer and gladness shall come into their sad and broken hearts.

"The war in Europe is over, but we have still to face a

powerful, cruel, and fanatical foe, unwarned by the fate of Germany and Italy. That war in the Pacific will be won as surely as the war in Europe has been won, but it will be won by the valor and suffering and death of our young men; and when Victory day comes for the Pacific we shall think of thousands of our young men who will not return, who will be sleeping under the long rows of crosses on the islands of the sea and on the shores of Asia, with the surges of the Pacific sounding their eternal requiem.

"When we think of that hard war yet to be fought and won, let us ask Almighty God to give us courage and strength and grace to persevere unto the end, and let us pray that He will send His Holy Spirit to heal the deep, deep wounds of the nations."

When I went to the First Church in Pittsburgh, although I was to have two assistant ministers and a numerous staff, I determined that I would not slacken in my habit of pastoral calling, but girded up my loins and did as I had done in Paterson and Philadelphia, for preaching without calling and coming in contact with people is an academic work. I recall what Robert Knowles, minister of the Presbyterian Church at Galt, Canada, and author of a best-selling book of that time, *St. Cuthbert's,* told me when I asked him if he did any pastoral calling. "Yes," he said, "I do, for I feel that before I preach I must irrigate my soul with the joys and sorrows of my people." So I have always felt, and so I have always tried to do. With membership several times the size of my former congregations, it was, of course, not possible to make a complete visitation every year, as I had done before; but I did as much as I could, sometimes taking one of the elders with me, sometimes one of the assistant ministers, and often going alone, both by day and by night.

One call in particular stands out in a pleasant and amusing light. On a February afternoon, in company with one of my assistants, the Rev. James Blackstone, now minister of the Community Church at Palm Springs, California, I set out on a round of calls in one of the remoter sections of the city. We started early and were making good headway, finding most of the people at home. As the afternoon wore on, we became interested in seeing how many calls we could make that day. At length, when the number was about twelve or fourteen, we stopped at a humble home, where, as a rule, the most pleasant calls are made. It was an easy call, for the woman, a fine elderly English lady, did all the talking and relieved us of any effort. We sat down before an open fireplace where coals were burning on the hearth, the woman on the right, Mr. Blackstone in the middle, and I at the left, with the cat sleeping between us. A little weary after the long afternoon of calling, and lulled by the glow and warmth of the fire and the pleasing musical monologue of our hostess, I presently fell into a deep slumber. Hitherto our friend had been talking generalities, something about her life in England; but, unfortunately, she suddenly directed a question point blank at me. Mr. Blackstone took in the situation, and made a desperate effort to avoid disaster by calling out, "Doctor!" Whereupon I opened my eyes, looked about me, on the woman, the fireplace and the cat, and said to Mr. Blackstone, "How many, Jimmy?" I was evidently thinking of the number of calls we had made. My remark was an altogether irrelevant answer to the woman's question, but she, unperturbed, went along again with the music of her conversation, while Mr. Blackstone and I sought to hide our mirth by stroking the sleeping cat.

Aside from the science of pastoral calling, the incident was a rather striking illustration of how the mind works, and how it likes to finish what it has begun. One of the best-authenticated stories of Abraham Lincoln's youth at Gentryville, Indiana, is that of how one day when he was driving a horse on its round at the mill as it was grinding out the meal, he would strike the horse with a switch which he held in his hand, saying as he did so, "Get up, you lazy old gray mare!" But one time, when he had got as far as "Get up," the mare lifted her heels and kicked him on the head. After some minutes he regained consciousness, and the moment he did so completed the sentence which had been interrupted by the mare's hoofs, ". . . you lazy old gray mare!" So, when we were about to make the last call, I had been thinking and talking about the record we were going to set for that afternoon, and when I awakened out of my fireside slumber, that was the word that was immediately upon my lips. Thus worketh the mind.

The Western Pennsylvania country is unsurpassed for beauty and charm, especially in the autumn when the forests are dressed in all their gorgeous colors, as Solomon in all his glory was not arrayed. As soon as one leaves behind the mills and factories and locomotives and steamboats and gets into the fields and the woods, one is in a different world. On days off I liked to drive up to our church camp, first at Indian Creek, then at Somerfield, on the upper waters of the Youghiogheny, almost on the Mason and Dixon line; and then at Ligonier, in Westmoreland County. But best of all, because of boyhood memories, I liked to drive to Beaver County, through the "South Side," around Hookstown, and the old river and ferry villages, Georgetown and Shippingport, and then across the Ohio, sometimes by one of the old wire ferries, to Beaver, where I had served a newspaper apprenticeship after I left college, and back of Beaver to Salem, Blackhawk, Darlington, New Galilee and Wampum, usually stopping on the way back at Beaver Falls, visiting my old home, Fern Cliffe, and Geneva College. These trips, both sad and sweet, sweet because of the memories of childhood, sad because of voices heard no longer and faces which smiled not again upon me, refreshed the mind and cleansed the heart. It was Jean Paul Richter who said that "recollection is the only Paradise from which we cannot be turned out."

I inherited from Dr. Alexander, my predecessor, a wonderful group of weekday and week-night meetings and clubs, most of them for women: the Mothers' Club, the Thursday Noon and Thursday Night Clubs for Business Women, and the Thursday Sewing, in addition to the Boys and Girls Clubs. When I suggested that we ought to have a men's meeting of some sort, the general reaction was that such a meeting would not succeed. They said, "You can get women out for these weekday meetings, but not men. They won't come." Nevertheless, I decided to make the venture. At the first Tuesday Noon Meeting for Business Men, held on the first Tuesday of November, 1930, twelve men showed up. But "despise not the day of small things." At first I had visiting ministers speak; but they came to the meeting cold, and unfamiliar with the atmosphere. It meant a new face and a new voice every week. After a few months I took the meeting over myself, speaking every Tuesday. In that way I got to know the men and they got to know me. The general plan of the meeting has been the same from the very beginning. Luncheon is served in the cafeteria as early as eleven-thirty, and also after the meeting until one-thirty. The meeting commences with hearty singing of the old hymns at twelve-twenty-five. At twelve-thirty-five the large male chorus, with many church choir singers in it, renders a number. At twelve-forty I speak, usually for ten minutes, never more than fifteen. These addresses are straight-forward Gospel and Scriptural messages, but always adapted to the daily battle of the soul. It is a kind of speaking and preaching that is quite different from the more formal pulpit sermons, and there is a certain ease and freedom of speech which makes it a delight to the speaker.

From that small beginning of twelve men in 1930, the

Tuesday Noon Club has grown steadily, until now it has a membership of two thousand, and a weekly average attendance of over eight hundred men. Thus it is the largest stated men's meeting of its kind in the country. All denominations are represented by the men who come, and we have some Jews and Roman Catholics. Indeed, the best letter I have received from any of the men, telling of the benefits and spiritual help derived from the meetings, came from a devout Roman Catholic. Wherever I go now I am generally accosted by some man who stops me and tells me that when in Pittsburgh he was a "Tuesday Nooner." Truly we can say of this Tuesday Noon Club, its "line is gone out through all the earth, and their words to the end of the world." To speak every Tuesday, from the first of October until the first of May, entails a heavy burden on the preacher, who by Tuesday is hardly over the strain of his Sabbath work, and has Wednesday's service ahead of him; but there is a great thrill and inspiration in addressing so large a body of men.

In all my churches I have emphasized the Sunday evening service, and in Pittsburgh, as in Philadelphia and Paterson, I have been blessed with large and enthusiastic congregations. The series of sermons are always well advertised in advance, in the weekly church calendar, by special cards, and also in the newspapers. There is always a certain advantage in preaching serial sermons, for there is a natural curiosity on the part of people, and a natural desire to know what the next sermon will be. In recent years I added a new feature to our Sunday evening service, the "Hymn Sing" in the chapel following the regular service. Large numbers come in to this gathering, for the people like to sing the old hymns. It gives an opportunity, too, for friendly greeting and social intercourse. After a half hour of singing, light refreshments are served. The more a church is open, the more meetings and services which are held, especially in a church like the First Church of Pittsburgh, in the very heart of the city, the better it will be for the church, the preacher, and the people who may come. We have now five regular week-day services, in addition to the stated services on Sunday: the Tuesday Noon Club for Business Men, the Wednesday noon and the Wednesday night services, the Mothers' Club on Wednesday afternoon, and the Thursday Noon Meeting for Business Women. At all the other clubs, and night meetings also, the devotional service takes a prominent part.

When asked how I manage to speak as many times as I do, always twice on Sunday, as well as presiding over the large Sunday School, always at Tuesday noon, generally once on Wednesday, and sometimes at the other meetings, my answer is, first of all, that I have back of me many years of experience and an accumulation of material; and, second, the habit of concentration, and also putting the work of my own church above the many opportunities and invitations to speak and preach elsewhere. It is a great thing for the preacher if he likes to preach in his own pulpit more than anywhere else. I have learned by experience to say No to nearly all the invitations which come to speak and preach in different places over the country, and, except in the summer vacation, I am rarely away from my own pulpit.

I have never wasted much time weeping and lamenting over the many divisions and denominations of the Protestant Church. This I know is in contrast with not a few of my brethren in the ministry whose stock in trade is the theme of church unity, and who seem to regard it as the great achievement which will solve all the problems of Christianity. This I have always felt is a great mistake. The Protestant Church exerted its greatest influence and made its strongest witness to Christ when its various denomina-

213

tions were strongest. The mere fact that two denominations or two churches are merged and become one, does not necessarily mean that the Kingdom of Christ has been strengthened and extended. Not infrequently it means that there are fewer workers in the various organizations and societies of the church than there were before, and sometimes fewer worshipers. Let no one imagine that Satan is much disturbed when he learns that two churches have been merged or that two denominations are now one. When that happens, the work of the church is just as difficult as it was before, and Satan's opposition to that work is unchanged.

The great peril in some of the movements of today looking toward a consolidation of Protestant bodies is the danger of effecting union by ignoring certain fundamental convictions. It was John Calvin who said that he would cross seven seas for the sake of church unity, and we all ought to pray and work that Christ's seamless robe shall again be one; but not at the price of doctrinal indifference, or when the impression is created that many of the truths which denominations have emphasized are of little significance. Many years ago, when in London, I worshiped in the King's Way Congregational Church. The minister was Dr. William Edwin Orchard, who afterwards went over to Rome, but who at that time, in answer to the attacks made on him for his Romanizing tendencies, stoutly affirmed that he would never become a Roman Catholic. In the sermon he preached that afternoon, he was on the subject of church unity. In the course of his sermon he described, in a somewhat amusing way, the attempt of two churches or denominations to unite. They discover that they disagree as to doctrine after doctrine, and practice after practice. Finally, since there is no other way of accomplishing the end desired, they unite upon the platform of the multiplication table, upon which all are agreed!

Abraham Lincoln, with his usual insight and common

sense, made a still timely deliverance on this subject of church unity. One of his friends was lamenting the divided condition of Protestantism and the number of churches; but Lincoln told him that there was no occasion for his lamentation. This is what he said:

> "My good brother, you are all wrong. The more sects we have, the better. They are all getting somebody in that the others could not; and even with the numerous divisions, we are all doing tolerably well. . . .
>
> "What we need is not fewer sects or parties, but more freedom and independence for those we have. The sects are all right . . . and should hammer away until they reach the best that is attainable . . . Think of what the sects drilling so many of us have passed through, mostly to our advantage as responsible beings. Our people came from the good old Quaker stock, through Pennsylvania, Virginia and Kentucky. Circumstances took us into the Baptist sect in Indiana, in which several of our people have remained. While there, a good Methodist elder rode forty miles through a winter storm out of his way to preach my mother's funeral sermon at Spencer Creek. Here in Illinois, we are with the Presbyterians, where the Methodists are as thick as bees all about us."

In my Pittsburgh ministry I began to emphasize more and more the printed word. Every month several sermons were printed in pamphlet form, distributed to the Sunday congregations, and sent out with the church magazine, "First Church Life," to persons all over the world. In this way the message spoken in the pulpit has been broadcast and has had a far wider hearing and influence.

Sometimes I am asked how I have been able to direct

the activities of a great church and at the same time write so many books, both in the religious and in the historical field. My answer is that the religious books, for the most part sermons, have been in the regular routine of my work and study. The historical books, of course, are more of an avocation, and required considerable research and travel. But by concentration, by devoting periods of the day to study and writing, in season and out of season, I have been able to get out these books. I have often said to myself, and to others, that the main thing is to start, to "get at it," whether it be a sermon or a book.

My first published article was the story of an encounter with a mountain lion in the San Bernardino Mountains in California; mostly fiction, but with some background of fact. I wrote it when I was a senior at the University of Wisconsin, and it was published in the Chicago Inter Ocean, then one of the great dailies in the Middle West. For this I received my first money for anything I have written, fifteen dollars.

My first book was *A History of the First Presbyterian Church of Paterson, New Jersey.* There was a great deal of human interest in the story of the century-old church, and I took much delight in going through its chronicles. My next effort, a drama, or play, centering about John Brown of Harper's Ferry, was never published. There are great possibilities in that theme, and I may return to it again. My second book was published soon after I went to Philadelphia. It was a booklet on "The Minister's Son," a record of the achievements of the sons of the manse. It was dedicated to Woodrow Wilson, then President, and son of a Presbyterian minister. This was followed by my first full-sized religious book, *The Parables of the Old Testament.* It was a study of those grand old tales of the Old Testament, such as David and the Ewe Lamb, the Woman of Tekoah, the Thistle and the

Cedar, and the Lost Prisoner, all much neglected by modern preachers and religious writers, as, indeed, is the whole of the Old Testament. *Parables of the Old Testament* was followed by *Twelve Great Questions About Christ,* published at the time of the great theological discussion, 1923-25, and dealt with the cardinal truths of the Christian revelation.

My first book in the historical field was *Lincoln and His Generals,* a study of Lincoln in his relationship with the various commanders of the Union armies in the Civil War. From boyhood I had intense interest in the Civil War. In the old American Encyclopedia in my father's library, I had read eagerly the stirring account of the Battle of Gettysburg. In 1910 I made the first of many pilgrimages to the battlefields of the Civil War, and since then I have visited all the major fields of conflict. The result of these expeditions was the book, *Highways and Byways of the Civil War,* an account of the battles, and a description of the fields as they are today. Other books in the field of the Civil War followed from time to time: *Lincoln and His Cabinet, Little Mac—the Life of General George B. McClellan, Lincoln and the Bible, Grant and His Generals,* and *Mr. Lincoln's Admirals.* The history of Western Pennsylvania, very important in the making of the nation, always held my interest, and my three little books, *Not Far from Pittsburgh, Right Here in Pittsburgh,* and *Where the Rivers Meet,* deal with the places and personalities of that part of Pennsylvania. Ever since I heard my brother Robertson deliver a college oration on Napoleon I had a keen desire to know more about him. One of the by-products of this study was the book *The Bonapartes of America,* written in collaboration with Major Gordon Dorrance.

When I was at Paterson I held a Wednesday afternoon vesper service, at which I preached a brief sermon, and when we had good music by different New York church soloists.

But on Wednesday evenings I conducted a men's Bible class, where we studied the life, the travels, and the writings of St. Paul. The class was small, but we did thorough work, and it was in that Wednesday night class, rather than in the theological seminary, that I laid the foundations of my knowledge of the great apostle, an unfailing source of interest and inspiration in my preaching. These studies bore fruit in my book, *Paul the Man*.

In 1925, when I visited at Rome St. Paul's Outside The Walls, and the crypt where Paul's dust reposes, I first conceived the desire and plan to follow in Paul's footsteps and visit every place where the New Testament says he went. That summer I had my first opportunity to commence these journeys in Italy and in Spain. We have no record of Paul's journeys in Spain, but we know from his letter to the Romans that he purposed to go to Spain, and there is a fairly trustworthy tradition that he did visit Spain. Since then I have made nine journeys to the Mediterranean country and the Near East, following in the footsteps of the great apostle. Some of these journeys, especially those in Asiatic Turkey, involved considerable hardship and some risk. On foot, on horseback, by train, by steamer, by donkey, by airplane and by chartered schooner, on remote islands, and in now wild and desolate solitudes these journeys were accomplished. My letters written on these expeditions are ready for the press, but publication has been postponed with the hope that I shall be able to visit first the few places to which I did not get. These are few indeed: Caesarea, on the Palestinian Coast, where Paul was in prison for three years and where he preached to Felix, Agrippa and Festus; Troas, or Troy, where he had his vision of the man from Macedonia; Amphipolis, where he stopped on his journey from Philippi to Thessalonica, and Perga of Pamphylia, on the southern coast of Asia Minor. I did get to Attalia, the port from which

Paul and Barnabas sailed on their return journey from the uplands of Asia Minor. Perga is only twenty miles from Attalia, and I looked wistfully in that direction as my ship was leaving Attalia; but I had no means of getting there; and, had I left the little ship on which I was traveling, I might have waited a long time before I saw again the Statue of Liberty. In these journeys in the footsteps of St. Paul, I came frequently upon the trail of St. John also: at Patmos, at Ephesus and the others of the Seven Churches, many of which John must have visited; Ephesus for certain, and no doubt Smyrna and others; and some of which Paul certainly did visit, for the roads which we know he traveled passed through some of them, Philadelphia, Lydia, Thyatira, Pergamos and, of course, Ephesus. It is my thought to combine the account of my visits to the Seven Churches with the story of my pilgrimage in the footsteps of St. Paul.

It was at Paterson that I preached my first "Sermons from Life." This was the event which suggested such a series. I was in my study one cold winter night when a caller was announced. When I went down I found a middle-aged, well-dressed man waiting for me, and evidently greatly agitated. He said Bishop McDowell of the Methodist Church, who had known me at the University of Denver, had given him my name, with the thought that perhaps I might be able to help him. Then he told me his story. He had married a year or two before an attractive woman much younger than himself. Business reverses had come, and they had to give up their home. His wife had gone with friends and had taken an office position in New York. He was now re-established in his business and ready to set up his home again, but his wife refused to return to him. He was sure that she had become fond of her employer, and that that was the reason she would not return to him. She was at that time living with members of the First Church in a downtown apartment house, and on that ground he pled with me to go and talk with her. It was a difficult and delicate assignment, and, for the benefit of some young minister who reads this chapter, let me say that in such matters we cannot be guided by sentiment alone, or by desire to help alone, but must, as far as possible, be sure that our taking part in an unhappy affair like this will not do more harm than good. I was not sure of this, but the man's distress was so great that I finally consented to go and talk with his wife.

We went down to the apartment, and, while he paced up and down on the sidewalk, I went up and talked with his wife, a most attractive young woman. It was clear from the first that she had lost whatever love she had ever had for her husband and was determined not to return to him. In as tactful a way as possible I said something about the obligations of marriage and then had prayer with her. As I rose and started for the stairs, she said to me, "I believe everyone has the right to be happy." When I came down I told the distressed husband that he might as well give up hope of his wife's ever returning to him. It was clear to me that she had formed a strong attachment for her employer. So I left him. But as I walked to my home that night, and many a night after, that farewell sentence of the young woman kept sounding in my ears, "I believe that everyone has the right to be happy." Many months afterwards, I was going to New York on the train and sat down beside one of the daughters in the home where the young woman was staying when I had called on her. She opened her handbag and gave me a clipping from one of the newspapers. It was the account of the death in a New York hospital, under somewhat mysterious circumstances, of this young wife. At once as I read the clipping, there came back to me the words I had last heard on her lips, "I believe everyone has the right to be happy." Now this was the end of it! That gave me my sermon, and a considerable time afterwards, in a way that betrayed no confidence, I preached my Sermon From Life on the text, "He gave them their request, but sent leanness into their soul" (Psalm 106: 15). My proposition was the higher happiness, and how happiness at the price of duty and right and honor is always an apple of desire which turns to ashes in the eating.

Another Paterson incident which gave me a helpful Sermon From Life, on the possibilities of a second chance, was the following. There was a young man, not a member of my church, but who attended every Sunday night. In all three churches and all three cities, Paterson, Philadelphia, and Pittsburgh, I have felt that I have been pastor in a double sense, pastor of my own members, and pastor of the great number not members of my own church, but who came to the Sunday night service. This young man belonged to the Sunday night congregation. He worked in a shoe store, where he had the full confidence of his employers, and was given the keys to the building. Unfortunately, he succumbed to the temptation to steal, and, going to the store at night, would take out boxes of shoes and sell them. At length his thefts were detected and he was dismissed; but his considerate employers did not press the case against him or have him arrested. In some way—if I remember correctly, it was through the young man telling me himself—this matter became known to me. One day I received one of the customary confidential information blanks from a state-wide business concern, saying the young man had applied for a post, and asking me what I could tell them about him, his character, ability, industry, and integrity. For a long time I held that form in my hand. What ought I to say? If I told the incident of the stolen shoes, he would never get the post, and his step aside would be broadcast still further. The form was so worded that without any deception I could say what I knew that was good about the man. This I did. He secured the post and rose rapidly to a high position. Some years after I left Paterson I heard of his death. He had been elected superintendent of the Sunday School of one of the churches of the city, and died lamented by all. On the wall of the chapel of the church there is a memorial tablet which speaks of his faithful service with the Sunday School and the high esteem in which he was held. That gave me the background for an effective Sermon From Life on the Second Chance, and how one mistake or transgression need not be final and fatal unless a man wills it to be so. These, and other similar experiences started me on a line of preaching which resulted in the book, *Sermons From Life*.

I was at first somewhat timid about accepting invitations to deliver lectures at religious assemblies, colleges and theological seminaries; but finally I reflected that I had had some unusual opportunities for study and meditation and travel, and at least an average amount of practical experience. Hence, I accepted some of the invitations which appealed to me, such as Lectures on the Stone Foundation at Princeton Theological Seminary in 1928, the Ott Lectures at Davidson College in 1934, the Auxiliary Lectures on the James Sprunt Foundation at Union Seminary in Richmond in 1942, the Bussing Lectures at Western Theological Seminary at Holland, Michigan, in 1941, the Payson Lectures at Fuller Seminary in Pasadena, California, in 1950, and quite a number of others. Some of these lectures have appeared in book form: *Sons of Thunder*, the Stone Lectures; *Preaching Without Notes*, the Princeton Institute Lectures; and *Christian Faith and the Spirit of the Age*, The Ott Lectures.

A question which his friends will ask a minister who has served as long as I have, and which the minister will ask himself, is this: What would you change, do differently, if you could begin your ministry over again? What did you leave undone that you would now do, and what did you do that you would now leave undone? What different methods would you follow? If I had my ministry to commence over again, I would devote more time to prayer, meditation, and the study of the Bible, although my preaching has been based entirely on the Bible. I would take more time off, too, and not run the risk to health which I have run through too-long hours of work by day and by night. Fortunately, in all the years of my ministry I have had just one serious illness, and that only recently. If that illness had come earlier in my ministry, I might have derived greater profit from it, both in the way of taking care of myself and in the spiritual lessons of understanding and sympathy for others in their affliction. But the Great Physician knows best; and I can say concerning whatever pains, sorrows or afflictions I have had, what the Psalmist said, "It was for my good that I was afflicted."

Every earnest minister will think more of what has been left undone, or done poorly, of the lives he might have touched, but did not, of the mistakes he made, of faults and transgressions, than he will of the little he has done. He will remember what the Saviour once said, "When ye have done all those things which are commanded you, say We are unprofitable servants: we have done that which was our duty to do." Yet I have faith that "as the rain cometh down, and the snow from heaven, and returneth not thither, but watereth the earth, and maketh it bring forth and bud, that it may give seed to the sower and bread to the eater": so shall God's Word—where I have spoken it earnestly and sincerely—not return unto him void, but shall accomplish that which he pleases and shall prosper in the thing whereto he sent it.

Yes, there is much that I would change; much that I would try to do better, and much that I would blot out. But, so far as the general plan and method of my ministry is concerned, that is, preaching on the truths of the Bible, faithful pastoral visitation, wide reading and constant study and writing, and investment of time and money in travel, serial preaching, emphasis upon the evening services, and preaching without notes, as to that, if I were to commence over again, there is not much that I would change, for I believe that these principles of ministerial labor, tested by the experience of many years, are sound, and I can commend them unto other ministers who are commencing their life's work, with the hope that in following them they shall accomplish far more than I have been able to do.

But none of us has the opportunity to begin over again. Save as it may turn us away from the mistakes of the past, and cause us to gird up our loins for the future, such reflection is unprofitable. "What I have written, I have written." Now in this last chapter of my ministry I thank God "that he counted me faithful, putting me into the ministry." I thank him, too, that the majesty and glory of the Christian faith, what St. Paul, its noblest proclaimer and exemplar, called "the exceeding greatness" of the gospel, has never faded or grown dim before the eye of my soul. My favorite theme for preaching has always been the Penitent Thief, and I have often said that the greatest text of the Bible is that word of Jesus to the thief on the cross, "Today shalt thou be with me in Paradise." Now, in bringing these memoirs to their close, I take, as the expression and the summing up of my own faith and hope, those words inscribed under the portrait of the great Polish astronomer, Copernicus, in St. John's Church in Torun, the city of his birth: "I do not ask the grace which thou didst give to St. Paul; nor can I dare to ask the grace which thou didst grant to St. Peter; but, the mercy which thou didst show to the Dying Robber, that mercy, show to me."